# About th

James has more than 20 years' sale: salesperson calling fresh leads and ........ v⊥ or sales & marketing running multiple global sales teams. He has been fortunate to conduct business in over 30 countries, allowing him to observe sales and their associated models from multiple angles, operating through multiple channels.

His background is in science. Having completed his degree in Chemistry, he started his career in software and moved on to work in instrumentation serving the scientific instruments market, primarily focusing on life science.

The science of selling is James's passion, being intrigued by the motivators of people on both the buying and selling sides of the deal. He is also fascinated by empathy and building alignment within companies to ensure that people know what they're doing and to focus efforts on meeting commitments (made) for growth.

After just over 20 years in industry, James pivoted to found Gaido Scientific, a consultancy business, where he and his team provide go-to-market advice and services, primarily to scientific instrument providers.

https://www.linkedin.com/in/jamesdanielfrancis/

# SALESDISK

## SALES MODEL DESIGN

By
James Daniel Francis

ISBN: 979-8401244062

Published by Gaido Scientific Limited

www.gaidoscientific.com

To my wife, Tamsin

# Acknowledgements

I would like to thank the following individuals who've contributed to the development of this book.

Jo Rogers, my work mother, even 7 years after retirement she is still helping and supporting me. Jo was there when I started in 2000 and she has been helping me make sense of my muddled writing for more than 20 years now.

Scott Young, Gaido Scientific. Even before Scott joined the team at Gaido Scientific, he was highly supportive of my passion for the SalesDISK© project. He has been an excellent sounding board and reviewer of the book.

Jim Schumacher, Mark Sebben and Rob LaBelle. All members of the senior management team for which I was part of for 8 years. All of which were highly supportive of my move to consultancy, and all who provided feedback and food for thought as I developed the SalesDISK© model.

Eddie Wal, BWD Partnership & creator of the STRONGMAN© program. Eddie has been providing me training, advice, and coaching for the length of my career and continues to do so.

Ravi Kotecha, Gaido Scientific. Ravi has helped get the project from a series of word documents into a physical book.

Tamsin, my wife, who has always allowed me enough space to take my chances on random projects whilst supporting me and listening to me ramble on about content and ideas.

# Contents

# Chapter 1: The Origin of SalesDISK©

*Defining Sales*

In my time, I have hired many different types of salespeople, some established, some completely new, some for dealer channel management, some for end-user, and some for B2B. They were all classified as, and referred to themselves as, salespeople. However, clearly, they were quite different. So how can we define a salesperson and what is needed to make the sale work for our product, market, and customers?

We have title descriptions such as channel manager, account executive, regional manager, internal sales and so on. I could probably give you 10 different versions of an internal salesperson alone; some people even classify these roles as marketing, not sales. Some of you reading this may even be thinking of course it's marketing, but with so many things an internal salesperson can do there is no one correct answer. The bigger question is: what jobs need to be done during the sale to make it effective, repeatable, and scalable?

Attitude descriptors such as hunter, farmer, loan wolf also exist to try to segment people who share the same title however, these are a little basic and do not capture the jobs to be done in the sale.

Diving deeper, why do some salespeople only ever respond to leads while others spend 90% of their time finding them? How come some in sales know the products well and others bring in an expert? Some need to demonstrate capability in person, some by web, some by video, some simply rely on the product specifications on the web.

Of course, products and markets are different. You could be selling a single $5000 software licence, 1000 components at $500 each or a single $250,000 instrument.

Tactics and Go-To-Market should clearly be different; however, I've seen $250,000 instruments sold without a demonstration, 1000-unit components sold over the phone and $5000 software products requiring a demonstration in person.

Clearly, product value, pull and perception can play a part of this, but I have seen each of these examples fail as often as I have seen them succeed. For me, the question is: are these sales models' legacy, organic or designed?

1

Sadly, there is not a 'one size fits all' go-to-market strategy based on average sales price. However, constraints often force similar adoptions. For example, you can't pay an expensive experienced rep to sell 2 x $5000 licences a month - basic economics force either a cheaper salesforce or an alternative such as web sales.

I developed SalesDISK© to help business leaders plan the sale and drive the best chance of winning and growing their business. It starts with an assessment and asking yourself really hard questions over what you value, what your customer values and what is possible considering capabilities and constraints.

Along with my interest in the differences between salespeople, I was interested in varying issues in the alignment of sales with marketing and other departments.

Salespeople often come under criticism from various departmental heads. Some which do not understand sales, and others which were previously in sales for differing products, markets, or times. The main reason for this is the lack of understanding of what salespeople should be doing. To many they can look overpaid, comfortable, or even lazy. SalesDISK© helps create a clear vision and alignment across the company on how the business has designed the products to be sold.

Salespeople are clearly involved in each sale, but what about product or application experts, often considered part of marketing? When are they called into action? What about CRMs which really belong to all departments? What about installation, service, getting referrals, repeats? Who is responsible for bringing in leads?

Good business cultures work when people know their roles - they can focus on excelling at them. Many of you have seen or may even work in businesses which feature ambiguity or lack of leadership and mission. There is a fine line between freedom of movement and toxic chaos.

Some of you have seen the real benefits alignment gives when sales and marketing sing together; it can be truly magical, and the environments created by alignment are genuinely great to spend your working life in.

SalesDISK© helps create a clear vision and alignment where everyone understands their responsibility in the sale to help achieve the win.

For a long time, I've been obsessed with what is expected from the salesperson. Job specifications are normally poor and are used as a catch-all. When you ask managers what they want in a salesperson, they tend to list out all things they know about sales and not what is

2

needed to win with their products in their chosen markets. A large contributor to this way of thinking is the lack of a repeatable sales model. For focus to be applied there needs to be a game plan, a model, a recipe for the sale.

Now of course every one of your salespeople will tell you that each sale is different, that's the job of the sales team - they want to tell you every story of variation and use it as an example of the differing nature of a sale. It is the same as them telling you of that one time that Manchester United was beaten 3:2 by West Bromwich Albion. If they are playing tomorrow, who are you going to bet on? For the non-British audience who are West Bromwich Albion? Well, that is sort of the point.

Sales can be different but the game plan for the sale repeats at some point, someone tried to reach the prospect, could have been marketing, or a cold call. At some point a conversation happened, then possibly a demo, then a quote. Your first job is to work out what you want salespeople to do and really importantly, your answer can't be they need to do it all.

The fastest way I've seen to destroy focus is to create environments where there are not really any expectations outside of quota and to then attempt to set them remotely with initiatives as the mood takes you. Salespeople are often isolated units, they often work away from the mothership, and this distance (physical and mental) gives them both freedom and confusion. Keeping up with the company and its often-endless messages can be hard whilst simultaneously doing their actual revenue creation tasks.

From their first day at work their job specification is already outdated - people will incrementally change what is required through the launch of the latest ideas or programs. If this is not correctly managed the result is misdirected salespeople who try to either ignore or follow, to their detriment, the latest initiatives.

Some will argue that sales have the easiest of expectations to meet - quotas. However, quotas tend to be based on experience and desire, not potential. The classic example here is observing a territory doing $2M last year and setting this year's quota at $2.2M without thought of the potential or any transactional limits which may also exist.

Quota expectation is useful for the sales manager and salesperson, but is the manager really setting the correct expectations? Are the expectations fair, and have enough resources been applied to achieve the expectation?

Salespeople being at quota gives managers comfort but are we at, above or below potential? Are the people amazing, ok, or in fact poor? Sometimes salespeople are parked so far away from the mothership without a model to follow that no one can judge their actual ability in any way other than quota. In this way quota can actually become the worst measurement tool, hiding inadequacies and missing potential. As an example, a Salesperson who was perceived to be doing well came under pressure when COVID-19 hit in 2020, orders slowed - was it their region? No one ever really looked at their actions, and under investigation the market was being served and not grown. They had gone up and down over time as they serviced demand well below potential of the market, this would have of course been fine if the model was to service demand, it wasn't. As Warren Buffett said, "it is only when the tide goes out do you discover who has been swimming naked."

The person was, however, the poster child for following the micro initiatives set by their sales manager, they technically did what they were asked and believed they were doing everything correctly. They were not following a designed model - had they been, the problems could have been observed and addressed much earlier. They would have been screened, interviewed, trained all to a plan and any errors would have been highlighted early.

Further confusion comes in relation to the use of the term quota, It is important to all agree if you are using quota, target, or goal. For me if you are really using quota as it is intended, this is the minimum required for the business to hit plan. If a salesperson falls below this by 10% the business is no longer functional in its normal form, so the salesperson may need to go. If a salesperson is 90% of goal, this is different.

How does a salesperson feel if they are allowed to stay at 75% of quota? Either they hate their job and are looking for another, or they think the quota was stupid. If they think that, you can infer they think you are stupid. They will be looking for a job or finding a way to make their job as easy as possible so they can settle with their feet comfortably under the table.

Of course, the problem is that quotas are set in many cases to control commissions. There are various ways in which this works but as an example, imagine I am a sales manager and I want to hire a good salesperson. I've investigated and it looks like they cost $150,000. I have thought, or I have been told by finance, that I can pay a base of $90,000, so I need to pay them $60,000 in commission. I think the region is $2,000,000 so I will set the rate at 3%.

Maybe I put a sliding scale in to pay 2% on the first 75% and 6% on the remainder. Be aware that by doing this, you may set the expectation at $1,500,000 not $2,000,000.

One thing is clear: if you are in sales, you carry some form of quota. Everything else is simply advanced marketing or being an assistant. I'm not slamming these positions or saying you're not involved in the sale or in persuasion of prospects, I'm just saying you're not a salesperson.

Quotas are of course useful, but what they are not, is an expectation of how to do your job as it was designed, in order to achieve maximum impact. I can of course take a laissez-faire attitude and say, 'I do not care how you get to quota, that is on you'. This is fine and can suit some situations, it is also unscalable or leverageable. Imagine as a grown-up company saying, 'We let the salespeople get on with it, they all do it differently'. Are they doing it differently because they are in different markets serving different customers, or selling different products? If they all left tomorrow, would you follow their model?

Left in a model-less business, good salespeople find their way. I was one. I was left alone, all of a sudden the UK was leading the world. It wasn't the economy, but my model that was working. Of course, you need to let salespeople experiment, have freedom and try new things, I am just saying that it is hard to budget your businesses revenue when you leave the model to the salespeople to develop. Of course, you can do this, but your answer will be +/-5% of last year irrespective of how much you throw into R&D.

For those salespeople who find their way, also be careful that this does not make them anything other than resourceful and good salespeople. Many believe this is leadership potential, it is of course one trait required for sales leadership but only one. Best salesperson leading to best sales manager is not guaranteed, and it is a dangerous game to play. Having a sales strategy, a model, a plan, drives focus and sets expectations, and the good news is it is completely within your control. Without this in place, how will you ever be able to pick out where to support the sales team, who to promote, and who may be better in a new role more suited to their talents, either in your company or the next?

Models help explain the sale, how it is to be carried out and by whom. They also importantly set out what is not to be done, and it is often this that forces the focus. Like any activity, it can have boundaries but without clearly communicated plans people will revert to doing whatever they want fast.

With a model you also achieve simplicity as you are controlling the variables. If you observe problems then large diagnosis is not needed, it can only be your products, your people, your markets, or the model. To summarise, people are bad at setting expectations to salespeople in any other way than quota, which is a great but imperfect metric. Further, by poorly managing change they can cause even more damage. In many cases by trying to add focus, you are in fact adding confusion. Unfocused, undirected salespeople make bad salespeople, even if they started as good salespeople.

SalesDISK© is designed to help set the expectation between the salesperson and their manager, driving focus, and increasing their effectiveness, or identifying incorrect fits.

*Building Sales Strategy*

Sales is a high-speed ride, and you need to get off it occasionally to observe it while it spins. As a director of sales or business leader, your job more than others is to ensure that you stare at it with a critical eye. This is strictly a no-high-five zone - you need to be critical.

You spend so long on the ride that you miss things happening - things happen often organically, people come and go as do ideas and initiatives, all distorting your original plan. That is if you had an original plan. My plan when becoming a VP was to understand what we had and put out the massive fires, this is true for many of us and let's face it there are no honeymoon periods anymore – you're hired to make change, not manage. If you deliver change, you're a leader.

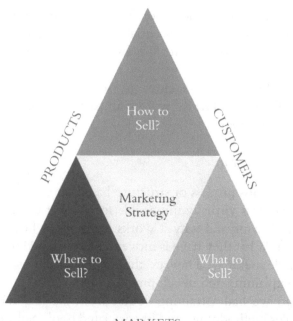

Figure 1.1 - Go-To-Market strategy triangle

What is a plan and how do you build a sales strategy? I like simplicity so I like to look at Go-To-Market using an incredibly easy graphic, the Go-To-Market strategy triangle seen in figure 1.1.

The Go-To-Market strategy triangle asks the what, how and who questions you will need to answer to go-to-market.

If you can provide solid answers to the questions posed, you have a plan. It does not need to be a great one to start with but one you can work with is excellent. As you can see this is more than a sales strategy – this is a Go-To-Market strategy, this means you're going to be joined at the hip to marketing and you're going to make the most of it. Operations and engineering will play a part, but your marriage is to marketing and all that it entails. This is simple, you both own the Go-To-Market strategy. You are in it together, both sales & marketing are going to control the external appearance of the business. Simply put, anything outside the factory or head office is sales & marketing. This is because anything a prospect or customer sees or hears about your business, is as a result of your actions and decisions.

SalesDISK© drives a large majority of the how to sell section of the Go-To-Market strategy. This is essentially what we are designing or recording to seek improvement. We are creating the manual for this sub triangle.

Although we focus on the how to sell section the shape and distribution of the SalesDISK© will be impacted by all areas of your Go-To-Market Strategy.

## *SalesDISK© is a Structure*

Many people dismiss process or structure based on experience - that is completely fine. It is virtually impossible for a golfer on the PGA tour to explain their swing and why it works for them or how an amateur can copy them. What they have is movement developed over time and stored in muscle memory. They are the player not the coach. Coaches specialise in explaining and developing.

20+ years ago we had a training course from Ed (Eddie) Wal who created the sales methodology and its associated book, Solution Selling: The STRONGMAN© Process. There are plenty of sales training programs out there, I liked this one and it worked for me.

The course was attended by 6 of us from sales including my colleague and friend Tim, sadly no longer with us. Tim taught me much about sales, he was experienced and was by now in his early 30's. He had a natural gift of not only getting people the correct solution but buying from him was like making a friend, possibly even discovering you had a cool uncle. He put people at ease and worked this key point like a master - people only buy when they are comfortable.

He was also king of what Eddie referred to as the "garnish" which was his term for simply how you ask questions or deliver messages through your own language. As Eddie would tell me, "Your job is to add the garnish". As an example, everyone knows they have to ask about timescales. You can of course ask "what are the timescales?" Or you can dress it up by asking in a less obvious way, "when does it need to be in and working?" It is the same question just asked differently. Salespeople often stumble at creating their own language to appear different or possibly likeable.

Tim and STRONGMAN© did not get along, he dismissed it as mumbo jumbo, unrequired and in some cases incorrect. He would argue against it as if it was designed to constrain him or undermine his experience. For me, a young rep in my early 20s, who had never done sales before, it was a structure that helped me plan sales and constantly assess what was missing and why the sale was not yet in. So, I had Tim, highly successful, sat to the right of me in the office, winning every day with the same products as me, and Eddie, an expert who presented me with logic.

Why did Tim not get on with it? Well because he did it automatically in his head anyway. His experience had formed the same connections in his brain like a golfer swinging a club. Every deal Tim was in he was running STRONGMAN© without knowing it. STRONGMAN© was not the answer to sales, it is simply a method to help you on your journey to the answer. There are many paths to the same thing.

Like Tim, there will be some who work on subconscious emotion (gut) and others, like me who need to get there using a structure. You can of course be correct with your first thought, even when making big decisions. However, if you are correct then spending a couple of days cross examining yourself, showing why you rejected other ideas and picked this one should not be much effort. In business you sadly don't get points for showing your working, but you do for selling, explaining, or defending your decision.

SalesDISK©, like STRONGMAN©, SWOT, and many others, is a structure, a tool. It's not the answer. It is designed to help you think, to get to a better answer, not do the thinking for you.

How is SalesDISK© designed to help your business?

- Review the main aspects of the sale so the management team can prioritise the important and outsource or de-emphasise the rest
- Identify existing, and create desired, Go-To-Market strategy
- Match the sales process to the customer/buyer journey, while working within any company constraints
- Create efficiency and/or effectiveness of the sale to increase hit rate
- Create a companywide vision of the sale where everyone in the company understands their position
- Help specify staff to be hired and identify where training gives the most benefit

So, what's your job in all this? What do you need to do while reading this book? You need to do the thinking, you need to do the personalisation. The concept is easy, it's pretty much covered in the next chapter. Everything else is hopefully thought-provoking, as any business book should be. You want to lead, you want to run a business or a sales organisation, want to be the best you can be? Well-read and think.

If you don't want to do it alone and need help thinking, then I completely understand. I recommend you do this as a team with other senior managers. If you don't know what to do next or need help thinking, get a consultant, get some experience, get a mentor.

I hope that you enjoy the book, and that it sparks thought for change for the better in your organisation.

## CHAPTER SUMMARY

Salespeople come in all shapes and sizes and their title does not really have anything to do with what type of salesperson they are or how their sale is supposed to happen.

Some salespeople need to find business - others only respond to leads; some demonstrate - others don't. Some do product installations - others do not. Some jobs in the sale may or may not be important for a salesperson to do and so could be carried out by another non-quota carrying resource.

Job specifications for sales staff are often catch-all documents which don't define direction or the job to be done.

Salespeople are easily distracted by the latest initiatives and constant messages coming from the head office. They need simple and clear instructions.

SalesDISK© is designed to answer the how we sell, part of the Go-To-Market strategy.

SalesDISK© is a structure for you to assess your own situation; you are required to do the thinking.

# Chapter 2: The SalesDISK©

SalesDISK© is a tool for assessing, planning, and implementing a sales strategy. At its heart is the review of the four key areas of the sale, referred to as segments - DEVELOP, IDENTIFY, SERVICE and KNOWLEDGE - the initials of these segments forming the acronym DISK.

D = DEVELOP       Development of Open Opportunity
I = IDENTIFY       Finding Customers
S = SERVICE       Post Order Actions
K = KNOWLEDGE   What Do Salespeople Need to Know?

The segments do not flow in order, it's not a process, you do not start with DEVELOP and then end with KNOWLEDGE - they are completely isolated, distinct characteristics of the sale and need to be assessed in isolation. DISK was just an accident of the first way I assembled the model graphically forming a disk shape and the segments names falling fortuitously in place.

*Graphical Representation*

The output of the analysis is the SalesDISK© itself which graphically represents the designed sale, showing focus weighted in the inner disk and tactics and deployed resources on the outer disk.
Figure 2.1, on the following page, shows a SalesDISK© with segments (inner disk) showing a clear focus on finding customers, IDENTIFY. The outer disk shows the responsibility of the salesperson to complete the selected subsegment tactics. The salesperson is responsible for 70% of the IDENTIFY tactics leaving the other 30% to be covered by others within the organisation. We can also see the salesperson owns 20% of SERVICE, 50% of the KNOWLEDGE, and 50% of the DEVELOP Subsegments.
By default, the SalesDISK© is viewed from the salesperson's point of view. The missing responsibilities and assignments can be displayed if needed.

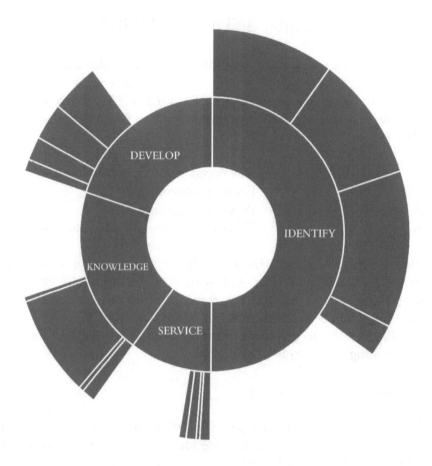

Figure 2.1 - Salesperson's view of the SalesDISK© - www.salesdisk.com

*Segments*

SalesDISK© starts with a review of segment focus, setting a weighting for the four segments (DEVELOP, IDENTIFY, SERVICE, KNOWLEDGE). The aim is to pick the focus needed by the business in its current circumstances.

An example could be of a new company, unknown in its target market, prioritising finding customers and so setting >50% of its attention to IDENTIFY. This is a clear message to any salesperson involved or planning on getting involved in your business. The job being specified here is for the salesperson to drive opportunity creation; in return the business is then de-emphasising or covering the other tasks required with other resources - applications people, internal sales, CRM etc.

Maybe a company is well known, often invited into the sale but failing to convert; here all effort is placed on the DEVELOP segment, focusing efforts on improving deal win-rate. Maybe your customers want a highly intimate sale and want to deal with experts who can explain needs - KNOWLEDGE.

Along with the company circumstances you may set the focus based on the need in the sale, as defined by the buyer journey or existing constraints. There are lots of factors which help set the inner disk focus and we will explore this as we progress through the book.

*Subsegments*

Subsegments can be considered tasks or tactics which comprise the sale. Depending on your situation some may be considered complex or simple. For example, configuring and quoting could be a multi-day exercise or a price sticker on a website.

Subsegments are optional, you can simply choose not to deploy them as a tactic - for example maybe you decide prospecting is simply not required within the sale or you choose not to provide installations. Finally, they are not equal to each other; quoting is not as important as demonstrating for example.

All of these options are highly specific to your sale. You are responsible for the assessment and just as with segments, subsegments need weighting to add the priority.

Unlike segments, subsegments need resources to be assigned setting the expectation for who will be responsible for delivering the task.

| SEGMENT | SUBSEGMENT | DEFINITION |
|---|---|---|
| DEVELOP | Listening & Positioning | Understanding and developing customer's needs. Positioning your product as a solution to those needs |
| | Configuring & Quoting | Selecting the product(s) and providing formal pricing and any additional information required to proceed through purchasing |
| | Demonstrating Capability | The act of proving that what you are offering works and that the prospect will be able to use it |
| | Deal Making & Closing | Creating the comfort with the prospect to close the deal |
| IDENTIFY | Lead Processing | Responding to inbound requests for discussion, information, and pricing. |
| | Farming | Outbound contact of existing customers in search of new business opportunities |
| | Prospecting | Outbound contact of new prospects with the intention of discovering or developing a need |
| | Business Development | Focused effort in finding new areas of business Examples: investigating new markets, finding alternative uses for products, channel development and expansion, etc |

| | | |
|---|---|---|
| SERVICE | Installation & Training | Completing the commitments of the sale and ensuring that the product is used for ultimate benefit |
| | Customer Support | Answering questions and helping customer throughout the life of the product |
| | Customer Engagement | Engaging with customers, ensuring their satisfaction, and obtaining references and referrals |
| | Warranty, Upgrades and Add-ons | Selling additional products and services to customer beyond that of the company's core offerings |
| KNOWLEDGE | Domain Knowledge | Knowledge of a specific discipline or field, for example – Software as Service, Test Equipment, Pharmaceutical Industry |
| | Territory Knowledge | Knowledge of the geographical region, the account locations, and customers within it |
| | Application Knowledge | Knowledge of job or task the prospect is attempting to complete having dealt with similar problem directly before |
| | Product Knowledge | Knowledge of your products, their features and how customers achieve their jobs with them |

Figure 2.2 - Subsegment definitions

Any subsegment task must be capable of being transferable to another department, another person, or an alternative technology. As an example, deal making could be done by the salesperson, sales manager, or business manager. Demonstrating capability could be done by a salesperson, application specialist, product specialist, product video, or testimonial, etc.

Resources in SalesDISK© are allocated across three departments sales, marketing and other - sales and marketing dominating as they collectively own the go-to-market strategy.

*Sales*

Any person or group within the sales department. This is anyone with a quota. Irrespective of the reporting structure, any additional help for the same sale would be considered part of marketing.

*Marketing*

Marketing means marketing, not marketing communications which is a subset of marketing. We are talking about all forms of product management, market managers, R & D staff, or anyone who would normally create, take to and care for, products in their markets. I also include in here applications & product specialists.

*Other*

Other can be a stand in for any other department or group, for example maybe you need to discuss a custom project where your prospect will need a deeper discussion with an Engineer. In this case Other is engineering. Maybe its service team, support, or management.

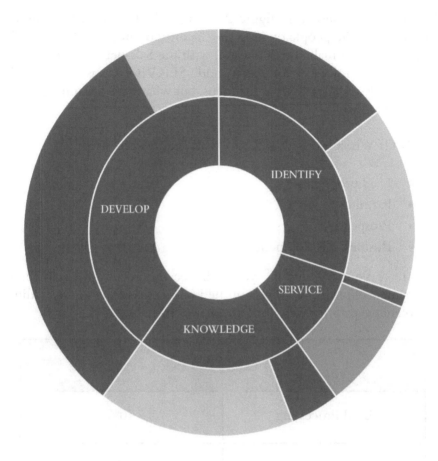

Figure 2.3 – SalesDISK© showing subsegment tasks allocated between sales, marketing and other.

In the example shown in figure 2.1 (page 14), IDENTIFY is key to the sale with salespeople owning the majority of this. KNOWLEDGE and DEVELOP make up 20% each, with the Salesperson owning half of the responsibility for each and SERVICE was minimised. IDENTIFY was clearly set as the focus, but what were the subsegments within that focus?

IDENTIFY is comprised of the following Subsegments

- Lead processing
- Farming
- Prospecting
- Business development

To create your SalesDISK© you will need to review each of these subsegments in turn, working out the importance of the job by adding a percentage priority weighting to each of them.

| SUBSEGMENT | PRIORITY |
|:---:|:---:|
| Lead Processing | 70% |
| Farming | 10% |
| Prospecting | 0% |
| Business Development | 20% |

Figure 2.4 - Subsegment priority weighting.

The example in figure 2.4 shows a business which has designed its sales strategy so that the sales team will have enough marketing-generated leads to support their goals. They expect some work with existing customers and some form of business development activities, which could be several different things.

Some jobs will be split between sales and another department and so we may want to assign a percentage weight to each job.

As an example, you may want to sell into a market or through a channel where only a few key relationships are important. If so, most of the responsibility for farming and prospecting may sit best with sales exclusively. Alternatively, if you have many customers and prospects, a working CRM run by marketing, creating call lists for an internal salesperson (such as products installed, or previous enquiries) could be more valuable. Here the responsibility would be shared between sales and marketing.

An example of an organisation which has chosen to service demand is shown in figure 2.5.

| Tactical Option | Priority | Sales | Marketing | Other | Notes |
|---|---|---|---|---|---|
| Lead Processing | 70% | 80% | 20% | 0% | Sales Focus, marketing to pre-clean leads but not contact |
| Farming | 10% | 20% | 80% | 0% | Use CRM, marketing to nurture |
| Prospecting | 0% | 0% | 0% | 0% | Focus based on servicing leads |
| Business Development | 20% | 10% | 90% | 0% | Marketing (product management) own BD sales assist |

Figure 2.5 - Weighting & assignment table IDENTIFY segment

Alternatively, the strategy for the IDENTIFY segment may rely heavily on prospecting as shown in Figure 2.6.

| Tactical Option | Priority | Sales | Marketing | Other | Notes |
|---|---|---|---|---|---|
| Lead Processing | 20% | 100% | 0% | 0% | Sales to respond to any new leads presented |
| Farming | 10% | 0% | 100% | 0% | Marketing to engage though usual tactics (email/social media) |
| Prospecting | 60% | 100% | 0% | 0% | Sales targeted on finding new leads – cold calling, social selling |
| Business Development | 20% | 30% | 70% | 0% | Marketing to create seminars and workshops – sales to assist adding attendees |

Figure 2.6 – Prospecting-focused IDENTIFY segment

Again, there are multiple examples for this. It could be a business starting with no presence in a market which cannot rely on marketing for lead generation, or a company focusing on selling OEM components into new unknown accounts or markets.

The priority and assignment are going to really depend on the customer/buyer journey, and how you align to it, along with any constraints you may have.

Looking at the 2 examples in figures 2.5 and 2.6, we can see that not only is the strategy to be deployed different but so is the job of the salesperson.

Job specifications for salespeople in these roles may in fact look remarkably similar on paper. This can lead to problems as salespeople from various backgrounds apply for the positions, which we now see as very different, but the job specifications aren't. This can at best waste time for people recruiting or those looking for work. At worse you hire them, and it fails.

You can never do enough prequalification of new positions or new hires, but on both sides, you need to reduce the risk. The aim is to avoid the new hire saying the words "this is not what I signed up for" or the sales manager saying, "I thought they'd be great."

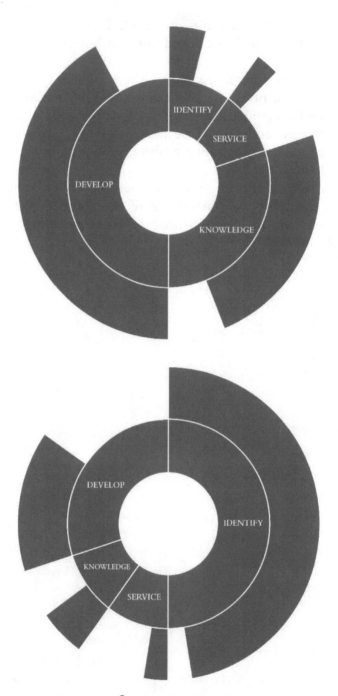

Figure 2.7 - 2 SalesDISK©'s representing the intention of one job specification. www.salesdisk.com

In the example shown in Figure 2.7 we can see two radically different jobs displayed as SalesDISK©s. One shows focus on DEVELOP and KNOWLEDGE and the other is focused on IDENTIFY. It is however possible that they shared the same specification comprising bullets similar to these.

- Answering incoming inquiries, discussing needs, and progressing to an opportunity
- Explaining the advanced values of products relative to application
- Building relationships with existing customers to identify new projects
- Developing business within your area
- Providing demonstrations, individually or in advance situations with product experts

Sadly, as no focus is set along with understanding of resources to assist the salesperson, it is clear to see that job specifications don't tell the full story.

Job specifications are like magical documents where whoever looks at them can see what they want to see, this is where SalesDISK© can help by displaying the focus, expectation and supporting resources collectively.

Rather than just helping sales, the act of creating a SalesDISK© and its associated data will help discussion of options to form or sharpen the strategy. Importantly, it delivers honesty for the salespeople letting them know what type of salesperson they need to be, irrespective of a meaningless title. They can of course not like it and leave, that is not pleasant and can be a distraction; your alternatives are allowing caveats or lying to them, and I have not really seen that work.

Honesty in sales is important. If you don't know the plan, don't reveal the plan, or lie to your people because you're afraid of what they might think they are going to do what they see best or lie to you. In such cultures everyone starts lying to each other and even worse they start lying to themselves.

When I started in a role about 10 years ago, we had quite a lot of internal lying throughout the global sales team, "Tell them what they want to hear and enough to make them go away" was the general concept, I may have even held that view on some items as head of Europe.

Japan was a good example. Every time I asked for a 90-day forecast the answer was, first 30 days bad. Next 30 days better but still bad. Final 30 days, excellent, problems over. No matter the month, the fix was 90 days away. It was the same as a sign hanging over a bar reading "free drinks tomorrow." They were lying to me as they had no idea what was going on. They knew it was not going to get better and so did I deep down. Neither of us had a plan but both of us knew it wasn't working. It was obvious that at some point I had to kick honesty in and make changes.

I want people to be more honest and this starts with greater honesty about expectations. Staff can't do it all so what do we want people to do? The answer is, do the plan as laid out in the SalesDISK©.

Sales leaders, make the SalesDISK©, hire to the SalesDISK©, train to the SalesDISK©, coach to the SalesDISK©.

The alternative is "See Brian, he is excellent, be like Brian." Ignore whether Brian has done it for 30 years, knows every customer, has the best territory, and failed a thousand times while you weren't looking.

I am not saying don't let your sales team learn from Brian, I learnt from many. Like Tim in chapter one as well as multiple others, just don't have it as the plan. Existing salespeople make great buddies and compadres, rarely do they make great coaches and trainers.

*Single or Multiple SalesDISK© Models*

The SalesDISK© is designed to represent a single designed sale, effectively setting focus and resources to be used, it is essentially the game plan, the strategy. However, some businesses are complex and may need several, as copying and pasting one disk across products, markets, or customers may not work.

Some businesses have a simple product line up with a relatively narrow price range where the cheapest product is 2-3 x less than the most expensive. If the products all do similar jobs, just with additional capabilities such as speed, quality, throughput, etc then one SalesDISK© is probably ok for your business.

This is pretty normal and easy to observe, walk into a car show room to see it in action. Take BMW as an example. The 1 series starts from

$30,000 and the 7 series from $90,000. They do the same function, as you pay more you theoretically get bigger, better and more prestige.

The sales model to sell each car is the same

1. Chat with customer
2. Push for test-drive
3. Discuss configuration
4. Chat with customer about finance
5. Look at delivery
6. Ask for order

I'm simplifying but I can't be that far off. Done well its impressive, I bought some great cars and enjoyed the experience. I've also marvelled at how some people maintain keeping the doors of their businesses open. You can of course argue that the salesperson wants to sell more 7-series than 1-series, that's fine and can be managed.

What about service? BMW car salespeople don't chase you for a $300 service, they have another team for this, mainly because it's another SalesDISK©. What about fleet sales where you are now selling multiple cars in a single transaction? The buyer is different; the test drive is needed but less important.

Product variation is just one example of where you may want to deploy different sales strategies and so different SalesDISK©s. Along with products are the other 2 main items that need addressing in the Go-To-Market strategy, namely customers and markets.

How your products reach the customer (channel) may also need a separate SalesDISK©. You may have different direct sales teams with different SalesDISK©s - for example, field positions versus internal phone/web sales. If you intend on using a dealer, distributor, partner, whatever you want to call them, they will need a SalesDISK©, so will your dealer channel manager.

Clearly in a world of infinite revenue and infinite resources you would have multiple sales groups and all manner of SalesDISK©s. What you can do based on the economics of your situation will be up to you. Compromise will often be necessary.

*Visualisation of SalesDISK©*

Tables of course are a great way of capturing and recording your vision but visualising a SalesDISK© helps paint the picture of exactly what is being asked of sales. It frames the decision, seeks alignment amongst the management team and, sets expectations with the salespeople directly.

The created SalesDISK© is based on a sunburst plot, which are available in Microsoft Excel. However, you are free to build your own or use the calculator at www.salesdisk.com.

*Next Steps*

Before we move on to creating a SalesDISK©, we will first look at the concept of trading resources. Here our job is to start thinking about what changes you could make within your business and to understand how your choices may affect other departments, especially but not exclusively your bed fellow, marketing.

Following this we will examine each of the segments in turn, DEVELOP, IDENTIFY, SERVICE and KNOWLEDGE. Exploring their composition and considering how specific tasks could be fulfilled.

## CHAPTER SUMMARY

SalesDISK© is both an assessment of existing/desired salespeople's responsibilities and a graphic that explains the focus and responsibilities within it

It is based on assessing 4 segments which make up a sale. DEVELOP, IDENTIFY, SERVICE and KNOWLEDGE – these form the acronym DISK and make up the Inner part of the SalesDISK© Figure 2.2

The Inner SalesDISK© represents focus whereas the outer SalesDISK© represents resources to be applied

SalesDISK© sees the sale entirely from the salespersons point of view, any job presented must be possible for a salesperson to do

Individual businesses will have different needs for the 4 segments and an assessment is required to set the priorities. This weighting will alter the segment distribution within the SalesDISK©

Resources in SalesDISK© are allocated across three departments; sales, marketing and other. Sales and marketing dominating as they collectively own the go-to-market strategy

A single SalesDISK© represents a single sales plan – all those responsible for that sale should be represented

You may choose to have more than one SalesDISK© for your business depending on the variety of products, customers, and markets you serve

You can create your own starburst SalesDISK© at www.salesdisk.com

# Chapter 3: Trading Resources

It's a funny expression, and one I've never understood, but there is more than one way to skin a cat. If you are a sadistic cat butcherer this is a useful reminder that you have options.

In a sales strategy design, similarly, you have options over the resources you deploy. The options you can trade are people, channels, and technologies. This is important as you may design the ultimate SalesDISK© but find it's not possible to execute due to existing financial or practical constraints and so you may need to trade resources to get closer to what you want.

SalesDISK© is about finding the best sales model to give the best outcome but considering your specific constraints. In this chapter we focus on the resource choices and the complexities that come with them.

## Budgets & Choices

1. People on different salaries are interchangeable, not always directly but certain aspects of one person's job can be done by another person on a lower salary.
2. People of similar skill set cost different amounts in different locations.
3. Some tasks required within the sale can be reduced in difficulty by using technology.
4. Salary cost is interchangeable with other costs - marketing, inventory, etc

Most people have a budget to balance - of course you will consider spending more if there is an opportunity which provides real revenue and is not just a mechanism to make it easier for the existing sales team (which can sometimes be the subconscious request).

New sales manager: "I want a add a new salesperson in the US - we need it."

Director: "What is the cost?"

New sales manager: "$150,000 in salary + commission – same as the others."

Director: "Well, let's add in some taxes, pension contributions, recruiting, laptop/phone, CRM licence, car allowance, travel – ok so $300,000. So really, we will need $1.5-2.5M to cover this. Is there $1.5-2.5M accessible in the market in the next 12 months to capture?"

New sales manager: "Errrrr."

In my career I have had that conversation both as the new sales manager and the director.

*Trading People & Expanding*

People have different skills and experience and that, combined with their current value in their local market, will determine their pricing (salary and compensation). You are free to trade different levels of people (experience, skill, location) to achieve your impactful mix in your sale.

As an example, in place of 6 experienced salespeople doing a bit of everything, I could have 4 experienced salespeople and 4 applications or product experts - it's the same cost. In this second scenario, salespeople must take larger regions but do less technical work like demos etc.

Be incredibly careful that for every resource added, along with expanding your effectiveness or efficiency, you may be causing more complexity as these people need to be hired, directed, supported, managed, assessed, engaged, etc.

This often requires extra levels of management. Adding more levels of management can of course be good - you get to give people a chance at managing others, providing opportunities to develop and, crucially, stay. Most people like any chance they can to change their title, show they are progressing, be rewarded, learn new skills etc. Just remember that they still need to be directed, supported, managed, assessed, engaged, etc.

Why did I say most people and not all people? Well, some people don't want the extra responsibility. Why? Well, there are a few different reasons - the simplest is they do not want it. They value consistency, work is a way to pay bills and that's it – they're happy. This is of course fine, good for them.

Another group exists that hides from it - it's an opportunity to get shot, don't raise your head above the parapet, you might get set up to fail, you might try and fail, and even worse, people might find out you were not great anyway.

There is one more group though, you may remember (it was a while ago). In chapter one I discussed quotas and I noted that if you set high quotas and let people live well below them, then they think the quotas are stupid, and they think you're stupid. Remember them? It's them. They have made their life comfortable and the company being great or bad is now irrelevant. They will live with your insanity - just do not mess up the life they designed while working for your business.

People fear adding management levels as they are costly or can be used as mechanisms to shift blame. This is of course down to you; most people want to add responsibility levels within their business. A good way to do this is to promote people to team leaders or player managers. This is part of a career progression and people like it. It's gentle also - moving people into management positions without living it a little first is harsh. If you do stop someone from doing their current role and give them a brand new one, you had better have a solid job specification and expectation. If not, you're trying to promote without a plan - it will fail. People learn to be managers - they don't become one overnight. You need to expose and coach them through the change.

I had one manager who hated the pyramid leadership structure - they wanted everyone to report to them, they dressed it up as cost saving, but it was really control. This flew in the face of everything I hold dear about leadership.

I've always been interested in the concept of leadership versus management. I see differing comedic posts in LinkedIn daily trying to separate the two normally demonising managers. I would consider myself a leader - I can manage well but I think I'm quite good at empathy and trying to work out what people are thinking and what I would want in their position.

I think my desire to be a leader kicked in when I was a reservist in the Officer-training program the Royal Navy had set up for those at university. We would go out on one- or two-week deployments on our training vessel, normally around the UK or towards France etc. It was a blast - tough but extremely rewarding. Never have I done such hard work, navigating, cleaning, and partying.

One day there was an exercise outside Falmouth, a small town on the British south coast. A helicopter was picking up students by wire off the front of the ship - a winchman would be dropped down, pick up one of our student crew and then winch them up to the helicopter. The winchman would then drop them off at another ship. All good fun, until, when picking up one student, the pilot lost his bearings, swung the helicopter left (port) taking the winchman and student officer firstly into the wire guardrail surrounding the ship and then into the sea.

Everyone was in shock. Our senior midshipman, our elected leader, was sick and we needed action. I just stood up and took over. I was 21, (everyone was 21- anyone could have stood up) and looking back I have no idea why anyone listened. I just said logical things with authority. I was promoted to take over from the senior midshipman as soon as we next docked. I should add that the incident turned out ok - everyone was ok.

So, I'm a legend - that's the story! Well, no - it's just the point I remembered. No one was doing anything, so I just started organising others - getting done what needed to be done. Leadership is so much more, but it does start sometimes with just getting up and doing it - taking charge.

*Leadership Levels*

I am a big believer in the concept presented in the book, 5 Levels of Leadership by John C. Maxwell. In it he presents the case that leaders exist in 5 levels of leadership.

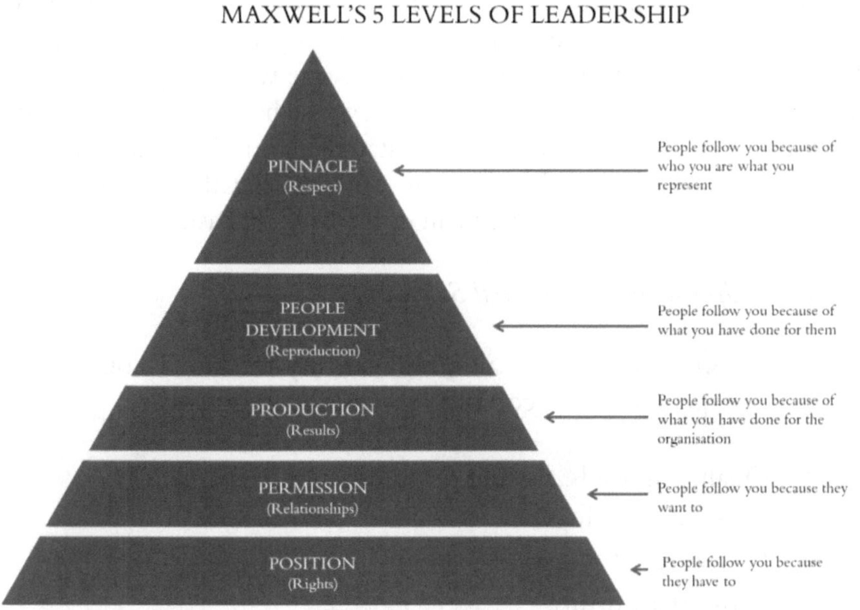

MAXWELL'S 5 LEVELS OF LEADERSHIP

Figure 3.1 - Representation of The 5 Levels of Leadership by John C. Maxwell

1. Position. Someone made you leader, so I follow - I must, I'm paid to, you could be terrible, but you are still the leader.
2. Permission. You are the leader because I must follow you and I want to follow you. You seem nice, have an idea, plan, etc.
3. Production. I follow you because I must, because I like you and because I see what you're doing and have done for the business.
4. People Development. I follow you because of all the things that got us to level 3 and the fact that you're trying to make people in your team managers and leaders.
5. Pinnacle. People follow you because of who you are and what you represent.

Clearly there is a lot more in that book, but that is the concept – buy it, read it. I really loved it because it made sense. I found that, after so many years in my job as a VP and a department head, wanting to be all that I could, I was focusing on level 4 - making new leaders. This concept is about building futures - society grows great when old men plant seeds for trees whose shade they will never sit in.

Help make people leaders in your business. You can create mini groups; they are not little houses of power - if they become that, you have failed, not them. I have found that people work well in groups of 4-6. They don't have to be teams - they just have to be mini teams with one person acting as a representative. You don't need to pay everyone loads more - they are the ones getting the exposure and training. If they do it well, they can come back and ask for more.

*Splitting Up the Sale – Internal Salespeople*

For every one experienced salesperson in my market, I could get 3 internal salespeople. They could do several different tasks.

- Qualifying leads, passing on to others
- Booking meetings
- Prospecting/ direct marketing
- Customer nurture
- Post-sale follow up
- Quoting
- Web demos
- Servicing low ASP sales

Internal salespeople used to be salespeople who were not expected to travel or be customer facing but COVID-19 changed this a little.

They also tend to be, but are not exclusively, newer to sales (less sales skills) and lower in KNOWLEDGE (all forms noted). These factors often combine, resulting in a lower cost. Their impact, relative to a more developed salesperson who can visit customers, depends on the SalesDISK© you wish to deploy. For some, if the business model allows, these people can be your entire salesforce as long as they have a good leader.

I am a massive fan of internal sales positions, no matter the situation. We used them to get new talented graduates directly into our business. They become useful very quickly and as the next series of talent coming through, when salespeople leave, you have options - they can quickly fill open roles.

I was one, my previous head of Europe was one, and my previous head of OEM was one. We were cheap, we wanted jobs, but critically we wanted to learn and were happy to do our time in internal sales - we could see where it led.

There is however one thing to caution you on and that is that they need you. You can't set them spinning and leave them. They need constant development, they want feedback, they need monitoring, and coaching.

Why? Because they've not done it before. By that I don't mean the job, I mean any full-time professional job. Of course, the best graduates did some form of part-time work - in fact without this I would not hire anyone. You can't get into your 20s without earning from doing something. However, they have never worked as part of a formal business where tasks are more complicated than simply serving the next customer.

What you cannot do is assume that they will run in isolation as a normal salesperson is expected to do. You're going to need very clear plans - support, check-ins, time for questions.

If you can, and your structure allows, and you have someone strong and good enough to manage and grow these people, I really recommend hiring graduates to take on these roles.

I should also be clear that you can of course hire experienced people to do internal roles - they are normally less needy, will have fewer issues with repeat calling, and they can tolerate rejection - there are some great ones out there. I personally love the open potential of new hires who want to try really hard and show what they can do.

*Splitting Up the Sale – Specialists*

As previously noted, you could use applications specialists - I've used them a lot across the world - they take the pressure off sales and also assist marketing. What did they do? Well, a number of things. They did demonstrations, they helped decipher customer inquiries for sales, helped with support, wrote articles, and kept the marketing content machine spinning. During COVID-19, when they could not travel, we exploited their skills for business development tasks exploring new markets and opportunities. They were amazing, truly amazing, nothing phased them.

They normally came from the edges of our key applications but were "wicked smart" and could learn products and applications super-fast. We hired PhDs and gave them their first job out of college - which had a few issues. The classic comparison being that although they could tell you how to calculate the volume of an orange, they just had no idea how to peel one. They just needed some nudging and practice to overcome this.

They helped the salespeople by taking away tasks such as demonstrations, manning trade show booths, giving talks to customers, etc. Some of them even became salespeople - this worked well as they had already completed all the product and application-based training we could ever want to give them.

There were some negatives however. Sometimes they forgot the game we were playing - we were selling. Even if you're in applications, you are still selling, just not as hard as the salespeople - but that can all be managed. Another negative is that they need solid jobs to do when not helping sales. If there are no demonstrations required, they don't just get to sit still and do busy-work like filing expenses. Their value needs to be extracted to get their full benefit and to ensure they don't rot.

I've seen plenty of errors with this approach. Some leaders believe that they have salespeople when really they have applications people who can quote, working to goals - in place of a quota. This is ok - if this is how you're doing it then your head of sales owns the quota, and their staff are just available hands to help them achieve their task. Having a region, being able to quote, being able to demonstrate, etc does not make you a salesperson - pushing your life to achieve more and win every deal, hitting or exceeding quota, even getting fired because of performance is being a salesperson.

*Dangers of Underused Resources*

Underused resources (people) cause more problems than they are worth. People can't just sit on shelves like tools to be used occasionally. People must produce work constantly and relatively consistently. An underused resource decays.

A VP of operations once told me that if two people in the factory don't look busy, lay off four. A bit brutal but he was correct - people who are not busy slow down the team. People who feel a lack of urgency in turn slow things down, and the observed becomes the culture.

Everyone employed must be outputting constantly. The results can of course go up and down as projects time out but people not looking busy are not good for business.

I have seen good people fail because of the managers they were assigned to when hired. Put simply they couldn't provide the direction or coaching needed to keep these people engaged.

I once decided to let two new applications staff be managed by two salespeople, one assigned to each of them. This was a mistake. The salespeople did no planning, so the application people had nothing to do when not demonstrating, they were resources on shelves waiting to be called to action but running idle when not. One of them stayed a while, became lazy, produced slow and bad work, and eventually I had to terminate their contract. The other, who was very smart, got bored quickly and moved on within 3 months as they couldn't see the need to be there. Ultimately this was my mistake, I should have coached the salespeople more and insisted on plans in place being instead of recommending them. Both applications people were good, the lack of guidance in the job rotted them.

Now this doesn't mean that people should all be flogging themselves to death. Some people will do a good 9-5 and some will do a good 7-9. Some will complete work over a weekend to get it done because they want to move on to the next thing. So how hard should you or your team be working? For me this is a matter of what you're trying to do at that moment, are you pushing to be more or do you just want to do your job.

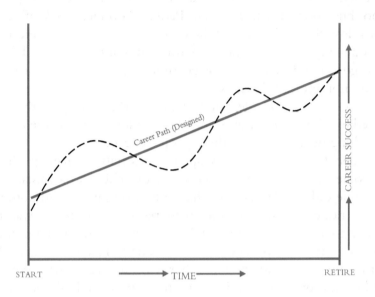

Figure 3.2 – Career success against time

Sometimes you push and are above your expectation and sometimes you fall below – maybe you can't keep pushing or have a life event, illness of you or a loved one, house move, children, etc. In figure 3.2 I plot time (X) versus success as you view it, money, position, self-worth (Y). A line joins the start of your career to the end, hopefully retirement. The slope of the line is for you to decide. Some may see their life now and plot a flat line from left to right as they want little more. Alternatively, some have it going up massively. This is now just a matter of effort and push. As I noted above, sometimes you're above the line and sometimes below as you push less or as the job you are in doesn't pose enough of a challenge.

I have lived in both. Under, once when having a child and the last time when the job I was doing just ran out of options – confined by the new management. Over (too many times to mention), working 8 hours every weekend and extra hours nearly every weeknight in my 20s and 30s, flying to different continents on national holidays pushing new ideas, pushing for changes and new processes, pushing to get people aligned, pushing my management to move things on.

If you are reading this book, you've made the decision to plot a steep curve - you know you're going to give some things up in your personal life, you know you must push to get to where you want to be.

## *Moving Costs Offsite*

You probably guessed this: people earn different amounts of money in different places. This is not only due to varying living costs but also due to the fact that resources such as talented people compete. So, if everyone wants someone in London then you pay more not only so they can afford to live in London but because you're in competition with others for those skills to be specifically in London.

I just saw a LinkedIn advert for an applications role in Life Sciences in California for $170,000; a similar position in Germany would be $80-100,000 and in the UK $50-70,000. In the same way, Birmingham is 40% cheaper for staff than London and comparisons could be made for New York and Indiana for example.

There are of course limits - the person from the UK can't commute to the US; however, in a digital world of web meetings maybe they can. In the past maybe you needed 3 people at a minimum to cover the USA, East, Central and West - if you don't need them to travel, they can be where the cheap talent is. Pittsburgh rather than New York, maybe Portland rather than San Francisco. Maybe they could all be in Milwaukee.

Even with travel, there are people who will happily travel and cost less. We flew people from the UK to the US, which costs about $1000. However, once we landed, the costs were the same as hotels and internal flights were needed for travel regardless of starting point. It worked but only for a short term as people can get burnt out. For many companies you can cover America from Europe and Europe from America - the time zones work out fine for Eastern US to Europe and vice versa. It does get challenging for the West Coast, but people can get up early or start late.

It depends on your needs and constraints- if you have limited cash, cover the area from your home base; if you need to get things really pumping, hire local people and push through. Asia is hard; dealer channel work is fine but it's pretty hard to navigate Asia at the best of times with direct selling.

For internal sales and virtual demonstrations, it can be very easy. During COVID-19 more than 75% of demonstrations for America and Europe were conducted from our UK office.

If you do choose to move resources to another country or use an office outside the mothership to save costs, what you will need is that person you trust to manage them locally.

I've seen first-hand offshoring work for internal sales, marketing, applications, engineering groups and service centres. I've also seen it fail - failure was always because of expectation and leadership.

### Spending on Other Things

For every salesperson I could spend X on......

I once turned to my president and suggested an awful thing. If we did not have Dave, we could have 60 demonstration units with customers running reviews at any one time - the cost would be the same.

It's harsh, I am talking about a person. I'm talking about calling a person with HR on the phone and explaining that we're making a change in the business and today is their last day. I'm talking about them having to have that conversation with their partner, having to look for a new job, putting their home at risk.

Harsh but true. I can spend money on anything. If I felt every employee in the company wearing a pink hat increased revenue, then we should google pink hats. The leader's job is to work out the best way to get the company to its potential. Ultimately the business must win.

Therefore, planning is so important that you'd better design it right from the start; alternatively work out what you want and spend time steering the ship to the new course correctly. Try not to mess with everyone's lives, but remember that doing the wrong thing for the business means you may end up with a lot more conversations with your HR lead alongside you on the call.

The role of secretaries is a good example of where we have seen technology replace people. Every time someone says my secretary will send an invite, I think about how easy it is to send an invite and how unmodern, slow, and lumbering that business must be. About forty years ago I remember my father having a dictaphone to dictate letters for his secretary to write. He dictated as he could not speed type on a typewriter; soon after, people got personal computers so they that could write their own; next, email made shorter communication easier, and then web meetings took over.

You may ask a similar question, why do you have all these salespeople, could tools not help replace the need for some of them?

So, what could you spend money on that would help you sell more if you traded out people for things?

The classic examples are

- Demonstration inventory
- Sales/customer/dealer meetings
- Tools – CRM, LinkedIn Sales Navigator, etc

Most of the things you're going to think of that have major impact are either going to drive lead generation for sales (marketing) or fund new initiatives in engineering and operations. Each department has a big spending list and more ideas than you can possibly imagine.

*Diverting Funds to Other Departments*

Would you trade one sales position for every remaining sales position being overrun with leads and crushing targets? If yes, then marketing's budget just went up and for sales, you just agreed to drop your headcount by one.

Resources are tradable and they trade between departments. I once gave up 25% of my annual sales budget to engineering. We reduced headcount where it was heavy, we trained new lower-cost salespeople replacing more-experienced, we shut some remote sales offices, we did everything we could. Why? Simple - we needed the money in engineering. Without the new products nothing made sense, I would have nothing to sell.

There were other things which fell into this, but we needed to live within our means, fund engineering and prepare for a better future.

Did I like it? In part, the challenge was interesting - some parts were very hard, particularly the bits where I changed other people's lives massively, however it needed to be done.

So, am I a nice guy? No - well kind of. Let me explain. As a vice president you are a member of the management team, and that's sort of it really. It's a team. Your aspiration of departmental power building is irrelevant - grow up. Your job is to win as a team.

If the products are late, sales need to make it up as best as they can. Why? Because it's a team. Teams don't win by going "well what do you want me to do?" and stamping their feet. They find the best way to work it out.

If your team cannot do this, or resists, this is really for 1 of 3 reasons

1.  You have not been listening
2.  You are a level one leader.
3.  You failed to make it a team

Being a level one leader is bad, not listening is worse, but not making a team is unforgivable. If it's not possible and maths says it's not possible, then listen and help if you can. If you want to say sort it out, or over to you sales, then you are not in a team.

If we had a problem with which sales required help to fix, I knew that the head of marketing, engineering, and operations would do anything and everything they could to support us. You don't have to endlessly high-five or love each other, you just need to be professional and understand that the goal is shared.

If ones down the other must pick it up. Team.

And critically if one department head doesn't want to help pick it up, wants to play games or worse, is constantly causing the problem, well it's the leader's job to act. Turn them or remove them.

So that's the secret - departmental harmony is Team.

*Marriage to Marketing*

I mentioned in the first chapter that your marriage in sales is to marketing. How you go-to-market and how you win is down to the two departments working together.

Marketing brings the products, messages, and promotion, they are not the goal scorers - sales scores the goals. There is an excellent video on YouTube by Gary Vaynerchuck, search for Gary Vaynerchuck Sales vs Marketing. He swears in it, my apologies, but it's great.

Chances are that you're going to show up in budgets together, you're going to see costs blend and merge, people can be debated to be on either team, the world is going to overlap on at least greater than 75% of activities - pretty much everything about a live product. They need you and you need them. If you don't get along, you're going to have to work at fixing this fast in the name of success.

At the very beginning of the book, I mentioned that some people have included internal sales reporting into Marketing, not Sales - this is completely possible depending on the job you want them to do.

If it is selling low end products, then sales; if its lead generation through prospecting, then I would say marketing. Sometimes it comes down to an agreement; if one of you is more capable, more interested and wants to take it on, that's for you and the other manager to agree on.

Product and applications specialists, who I have always loved, can sit between sales and marketing. They are not quota carrying – yes, you can give them commissions and bonuses but that's different, you can't terminate them over that (you're dressing it up to get to their desired salary, just be honest). If they are helping sales every so often then they are marketing, if the sale won't happen without them, then sales.

I repeat my warning - if you can't get on with the head of marketing and don't meet several times a week to ensure overlap, then I don't see it working to full effect. They are the closest thing you're going to have to a doubles partner in Tennis. You will speak different words, may have different objectives but you both own the Go-To-Market strategy.

*Spending on Technology*

People for machines - surely that's the dream. We all magically have more leisure time, right? This is what was promised to me as a child by TV.

The obvious change we have observed in our lifetime is the internet. For a long time, you have had the ability to sell online but many of us have avoided the buy-it-now button. But as Bob Dylan said "the times they are a-changing."

Websites that are used to provide useful information, assisting the customer as they progress their information search and even evaluate your products are tools. Websites for sales, transactions are channels. This is an important differentiator. If you use it as a channel, it's a pure trade for the cost of sales employees; if not, you're simply using a tool to make your business better.

Adding product pricing to websites will normally be hated by salespeople - even its accessories or low ASP products. Why? Because they hate giving anything up that could give them revenue - even if it's a distraction, a waste of time and something they consistently complain about. But done well and carefully, you can easily shift people to buying online, especially low ASP products, add-ons, parts, etc.

Alongside websites as channel are website tools like live chat. These tools help just as a sales assistant does in a department store - you can direct people around your website or fetch a person who can help the buyer. I'm a fan and want to see more, I'm even up for live people, people at a counter ready to chat, or show products just as if a person walked up to a tradeshow booth.

This is not a direct replacement for a staff member, but it is a change in required skills. Live chat use grew enormously during the COVID-19 lockdowns. Why? It was simply easier to get hold of staff online than waiting on hold on a telephone helpline. It has forced the adoption more; I think it can be a great tool. Technology doesn't always replace people - it mainly is designed to increase efficiency or effectiveness. As noted before, you have jobs to do, and you hire and fire resources to do them. If LinkedIn Sales Navigator means you can run fewer adverts, stop using the direct marketing agency or lose the internal salesperson responsible then you could dispose of those resources replacing them with Sales Navigator. Alternatively, you can keep or re-deploy those resources to push for more.

I also think websites are the presentation tools of the 2020s. If ever I am meeting a customer to talk to them, everything I want to talk about should be on the website. Most of your information should be accessible to all but some of it only to staff - that can be easily controlled. Sales staff tend to abandon their websites dismissing them as something for their customers and continue instead with pdfs and PowerPoints. The website is for salespeople as much as it is customers. If you have information, it should be on your website - again you can control access so customers can't see all of it. But why give people so many ways to access information? Have one - your website. You can also provide Sales staff with fully downloaded versions just in case they can't get internet access.

One thing I want to be clear about is that I'm not saying a website is the answer. In 2000 people believed it was – that if you had a website, you had a business. Now it's just an essential, like having a business card was.

A second point to be clear about is that websites only help service demand. One thing I hate is people thinking that they generate demand; as if we are all strolling along a near infinite street of website home pages and see an offer and think, oh, darling let's go in and have a look.

SEO (search engine optimisation) and Google AdWords are a couple of ways of attracting people searching for information directing them to your website. What they are not doing is generating demand only helping you service it, hopefully steeling the demand created by your competitor. Other interruption tactics such as advertising, trade shows, content, social media also drive people to your website. The trick is clear - you must drive people to the website. Oh, and to be annoying, to make it work you want the right people, as the wrong people visiting and running away make it worse destroying your SEO.

Lastly, we should mention the other web-based tool which made 2020 what it was, Web meetings. "Dave, you're muted again!"

COVID-19 has forced us to adopt live meetings more; we had the functions before but maybe for internal meetings, less with customers. Never turn your camera on though, oh no.

Then isolated, scared, confused we needed to see each other so, lights, camera, action!

10 days before the national lockdown in the UK, I walked into our office and made the prediction that we were going to face real issues; it was in the news but many in our business in the US were ignoring it as best they could. 10 days later we had 6, multi-webcam, fully operation demonstration stations, with people trained on their operations. Some of them were set up in people's home, taking over their living rooms. We were as prepared as we could be. Prospecting was still hard - we had customers landlines not mobile numbers. But we could do something, and we did. I have never been so proud of a team I've been associated with.

Web meetings are not trading people for technology they are just enabling a different way of meeting prospects which can cost a lot less than the alternatives. They create efficiency by killing travel time, they help funds to be re-allocated into more things you want to do.

So now, as COVID-19 hopefully starts to unwind (history will tell), will we go back to meeting customers in person? The answer is yes of course, but it will be less now that we have an alternative that works. Web meetings and demonstrations of products have real potential to be something else - green screens, lighting and editing software are all now so accessible. It doesn't have to be another boring meeting with Alan sharing his endless presentation slides like a stereotypical uncle sharing his vacation pictures in the 80's.

This is your own live TV channel, with people, real people. This is the future, high production values for all. We can all have our "15 minutes of fame" just as Andy Warhol predicted.

*Transactional Limits*

Salespeople, like all people, can only do so much - they will get hit by a transactional limit which, to overcome, may need you to reassess the sale and assist with additional resources. This is a good way to look at the sale, plotting out how much time each task is taking and if you're being reasonable in what you're asking of your salespeople.

This is normally how a decent sales plan is formed: "I need 7 deals of $25,000 each a month to hit my quota, therefore I need X demos from Y meetings based on Z opportunities." We are reversing this and looking at the time required to do these activities and seeing if we can pick better tactics for the salespeople to deploy.

As a rough calculation, a company operating on reasonable margins, greater than 60%, will need salespeople to bring in about $2M each; this means they bring in $1.2M in profit. Sounds like the salesperson is a legend until you think about paying the rest of the business.

This will of course vary - if you need to spend a lot on marketing to achieve goals, or spend more on R&D, or have high operating expenses, then you're going to need more. OEM or component sales in our industry would probably range from $5 to $10M per salesperson, in other industries they can be a lot more. The cost of sales is lower on the face of it, but so are the margins and there are some hidden costs like customisation and additional engineering resource. Clearly distributors live on much lower margins, 20-40%, but do not bear engineering or R&D costs.

Setting a revenue number by salesperson is of course a critical part of your business plan. Normally you need to consider a transactional limit based on your model - put simply, this is how many deals can they spin at once. For me and people I worked with, I saw that the maximum number of deals people could really stay on top of at one time was about 30. This was for products we needed to sell as a solution with lead-times of 6-10 weeks; for more transactional sales with shorter deal cycles, we could manage about 60. It's the same as a restaurant, they only have so many tables and depending on the number of courses (deal complexity) they may or may not be able to turn the tables on the night.

Let us assume that you have a complex sale – maybe lots of demonstrations required, with a hit-rate of 20%. Your aim is for each rep to sell 20x $100,000 units a year, making our nice $2M per salesperson level.

Because of hit-rate you are going to need to find 100 customers, maybe demo to 50, write proposals for 40 and then win 20. As shown in figure 3.3, this does not work.

| ACTION | ASSUMPTION | DAYS | RUNNING TOTAL |
|---|---|---|---|
| Working Days in a Year | Weekends, National Holidays & Vacation Removed | 230 | 230 |
| Calling and Developing Business | 100 days | -100 | 130 |
| First Meetings | 100 x 1 Day meetings | -100 | 30 |
| Demonstration | 50 X 1 Day Demos | -50 | -20 |
| Proposals & Quotes | 40 X 1-day Proposals | -40 | -60 |

Figure 3.3 – Table shows a failed model assumption where activities to meet the required revenue do not match the time available.

We can fix this problem in a few different ways.

| ACTION | RESOURCE | COST TO SALE |
|---|---|---|
| Calling and Developing Business | Internal Salesperson | $20-40,000 |
| Calling and Developing Business | Marketing Lead Generation Support | Unknown |
| First Meetings | Applications or Product Specialist | $40-70,000 |
| First Meeting | Build system to reduce or eliminate step, Utilise web technology | Unknown |
| Demonstration | Applications or Product Specialist | $40-70,000 |
| Demonstration | Build system to reduce or eliminate step, Utilise web technology, References, trials, sale-or-return | Unknown |
| Proposals and Quotes | Internal Salesperson or Administrator | $20-40,000 |
| Proposals and Quotes | Build system to reduce or eliminate step, Standard templates, configuration tools, make quoting easier | Unknown |
| First Meeting, Demonstration, Proposal and Quote | Training and Other Tactics to increase hit-rate | Unknown |

Figure 3.4 - Tactics which could be used to meet the required transaction level.

There are some massive assumptions made in Figure 3.4, firstly the cost shown are my estimates for sharing the hired resource between 2 or more salespeople. Secondly, we are unsure if the resources are capable of achieving the tasks.

Assessing the time and tactics in the sale is a good way to understand what is actually possible and not only where resources can be added to meet the desired transactional level but how do we go beyond it. If we really want to grow, we should be asking ourselves, how could we add resources to take the Salesperson from $2M to $3M or more?

## CHAPTER SUMMARY

SalesDISK© is a structure to help design the best Sales Strategy for your business. However, your business, like all of them, will have constraints - the clearest one being financial. The resources which you can trade to achieve tasks are People, Channels and Technology.

People do different jobs, they also get paid different amounts. Your job is about impact. What is the best way, or the best mix of staff, to achieve - given the financial constraints you have?

If you look at expanding your team by introducing or trading staff, be aware of the problems of scale and adding management levels.

Adding management layers does have the advantage that you can start to train new leaders within your business. This is step 4 in John C. Maxwells 5 Levels of Leadership.

Internal resources (internal sales) can do many of the tasks carried out by existing high-cost/high-value field staff. I strongly advise this as a tactic to any business that can afford to do so. However, be aware that they will need attention and development to grow; you can't just put them in the corner and say go.

Staff costs can be traded within business, sometimes for things that benefit sales, sometimes to benefit other departments. You cope with this by being a grown-up. This is because businesses work best when they have a clear functional management team.

The internet has bought us many things - one is web-based sales, but this is not the only thing that can be used to help sales. Newly adopted (although not new) tools like live chat and web meetings can help us further and, with data rate stability, we are all marching to become our own TV presenters.

# Chapter 4: DEVELOP

DEVELOP is the first segment we are going to put under the microscope and dissect. DEVELOP in the SalesDISK© model comprises Listening & Positioning, Configuring & Quoting, Demonstrating Capability and Deal Making & Closing.

| SEGMENT | SUBSEGMENT | DEFINITION |
|---|---|---|
| DEVELOP KNOWLEDGE | Listening & Positioning | Understanding and developing customer's needs. Positioning your product as a solution to those needs |
| | Configuring & Quoting | Selecting the product(s) and providing formal pricing and any additional information required to proceed through purchasing |
| | Demonstrating Capability | The act of proving that what you are offering works and that the prospect will be able to use it |
| | Deal Making & Closing | Creating the comfort with the prospect to close the deal |

Figure 4.1 – Subsegment definitions

DEVELOP is selling. It's the part we all recognise - talk to the customer, understand the needs, explain the value, demonstrate value, close the deal, easy. It is the heart of the sale - the juicy bit.

It's also the favourite bit, a classic interview and review question I had for salespeople was rank these 4 parts of the sale from most favourite to least favourite - find, first key interaction, demo, close.

Everyone always ranked demo and first key interaction as one or two, clearly people love taking the lead part, they clearly hate auditioning and learning the lines.

The key questions you need to answer are.

- Who is responsible for understanding needs and the customer position?
- How and by whom is the product capability demonstrated?
- How complex is our product to configure, quote and propose?
- Who is responsible for closing business?

*Listening & Positioning*

The adage says you have two ears and one mouth and use them in that order but it's amazing how often salespeople want to be a walking advert, presenting fact after fact, even handling objections which don't even exist yet.

Listening & positioning starts with need recognition and empathy. Empathy is probably one of the best things you can install in a salesperson. Understanding the other person's position and options is essential. This is where SPIN selling, and most sales processes help us to discover needs and to match your solution to them.

Some sales positions require virtually no empathy. The more you service a sale the less you need to understand about the motivations which created it. At the most basic level, I used to work in a fuel station. People purchased fuel and food. I knew they needed fuel to get their cars to their locations and food because they were hungry or bored and eating fills a gap.

I understood why I was there and the customers basic motivations, but I was not going to engage them with a question like "what kind of hungry are you?"

If needs are easy for everyone to know, like hunger or thirst then a salesperson is less important to the sale than marketing messages and availability. I'm hot, Coke adverts show people refreshed, there is a vending machine, job done. E-commerce clearly exploits this without salespeople ever needing to be involved.

In many cases needs are known by both parties and do not need to be developed or discussed and in fact the discussion is more of an irritant than a positive. In a world of mass information and branding people often arrive at a salesperson with their needs relatively clear. This is great if they have pre-selected you but for many suppliers, you may be simply a final gut check to make sure they are doing the correct thing with their initially selected vendor.

If the need is well understood by the customer and you, do you shut up and transact? Not always, the salespersons job should be to review and move onto check the commitment of the transaction. Why check the commitment? Because in many cases if it feels too easy, it is.

Maybe 80% of your customers arrive knowing what they want; if so, you need a service-based sales team. If your product is a market leader and it's uncomplex and transactionally easy that's fine. If it's complex and you have competitors of equivalent size, it may be that you are missing massive chunks of the market.

With complex products it has always amazed me how customers can arrive quite so prepared and specific, on needs. "I want a widget which is X micro parsons with 34% wiggle factor and 2.8 electrons of jiggles of interaction at the binary level."

Some know what they want through homework and reading; some are asking you for a second quote, having had the key first interaction with a competitor's salesperson. Either way needs go deeper than basic specifications and they include business and personal elements, if you can understand them, you can have impact in that sale and on your hit-rate in general.

I once had a salesperson responsible for selling >$100,000 products who could tell me no more than an application headline

Q. Why are they getting it?
A. They are doing Quantum research.

Q. Why do they want this product in particular?
A. They asked for it.

Q. What is it about our product that helps them?
A. It is the best, they want to do Quantum research, and this does it.

Q. What is stopping them buying the competitor equivalent at 20% less or our product one down in specification?
A. They want it. It is the best one.

I'm always amazed to consider what in fact the salesperson and prospect actually spoke about, how did they hold a conversation? I know virtually nothing about quantum research, but I would have questions like why? What are you trying to achieve? How does the product fit? Why did you choose this one? Isn't that just naturally taking an interest, like talking to someone you've not met before at a BBQ.

Now, the answer is that sometimes the person does just buy it. However, for every one that went well, I can show another where the answer is something like "oh, they got the competitor's due to some feature, mode, price, something they never mentioned to me." If you don't understand the need, you can have little influence on the sale. You are running an assisted purchase and not a solution sale. That is of course fine, if you designed it that way.

Understanding the needs mean you understand the deal and you can act on elements to build positions, prepare for objections, re-engineer solutions and provide options. Critically, if you understand needs you can drive the sale - increasing hit-rate, reducing sales-cycle time, and increasing forecast accuracy. I have always found that those with accurate forecasts sell more because they understand more.

That, by the way, is one of your needs. Yes of course you want to drive the business to higher wins, but you also must keep the trust of those who made you king, whether they be investors, shareholders, a holding company or your boss. Forecast accuracy helps build credibility with all.

Some salespeople focus their time with customers discussing application needs and specifications. For example, they want a product with dimensions X, Y, Z etc, by over focusing here they will miss the organisational and personal needs.

Organisational and personal needs are much harder to discuss, they don't flow as easily. I find the more intimate the communication mechanism used, the easier it is to ask these questions or simply know when its correct to ask based on the flow of the conversation or rapport built. An in-person meeting is easier than a web meeting, which is easier than a phone call, and of course easier than email where I find it virtually impossible to obtain anything other than application needs.

Most questions your salespeople are going to ask are going to start with the words what and why. For example, what are you trying to do and why are you trying to do it? But I'm not going to go into the questions to ask here, for tips for asking questions see sales-training and question development books. The only tip I will give your salespeople is to practice the questions, write them down, see if they are reasonable.

Your salespeople are going to need coaches to help them develop questioning, these can be internal or external. Some sales managers/directors can do it but that doesn't mean they should. Many, and I mean many really can't.

Often salespeople want to minimise questioning as they think that you only get so much of a prospects time and so endlessly listing questions has a high chance of irritation. However, asking questions should be part of a natural discussion, if it's not natural then we need to get some training implemented.

It is completely reasonable to ask questions if it fits the conversation. If it doesn't then of course they sit out of context, and it feels weird for both people.

High value salespeople are meant to understand and develop needs through questioning; it makes for a better low friction sale. The greater the empathy, the more chance of winning. Only through asking reasonable questions and listening to the answer can your salespeople ever get the chance to position your products. If they can't do this, they are advanced quoting machines to be replaced by lower cost internal salespeople or e-commerce.

Many years ago, I had a salesperson in the Midwest region of the US. They could not find a natural way of asking questions - they were what we refer to as a "question mark" by which I mean that we were undecided if they would make it. They had had the training and coaching, and something was just not clicking. I observed a few calls, and they would ask question after question like it was a survey, frustrating prospects because it felt unnatural.

The next step after observing is showing, so I offered to help by attending a web meeting with them and a high value prospect. I remember it well – I was in Japan at the time, it was a 4am web meeting and I was jet lagged and exhausted. We all arrived online, and I simply said, "nice to meet you, what do you do, why do you need this product and what's important to you?" He then spoke for the next 5 minutes giving me everything I needed, and everything my salesperson wanted to ask 20 individual boring questions to obtain. Your salesperson has questions they need answering, they don't need to ask them all directly and individually; let them talk and they will normally tell you everything you need to know.

Needs discussion and development is vital and understanding the job to be done within the sale is especially important. How much you need to do this and how important it is to you is down to your products and customers.

But who is going to do it? The salesperson, product or application specialists or could you use the website to drive out needs through messaging or self-guided configurators?

Salespeople clearly must own the questions relating to the deal but the discussion on the specifics of what is to be purchased based on application, may sit better with an applications or product specialist.

The salesperson can be a fully trained field salesperson with years of experience; equally they could also be a newly hired internal salesperson following a process. This is for you to work out.

Your salesperson may start the sale by discussing the broader needs and then bring in an applications person for more complicated discussions. Alternatively, you may just have a specialist help a new salesperson for a few months to get them up and running. Both strategies are fine. I strongly recommend you put boundaries on these tactics before you accidently create a two-person team doing what was intended for one. I have seen this happen and yes, we got the territory number, but we paid twice as much to cover that as we did in other regions. Sometimes they relax into a team, sometimes the salesperson is just not strong enough to pick it up and possibly should not be there.

If you select a model where sales pull in an expert, you need to make sure that this is designed in and is being utilised as planned. As an example, I've seen some people refuse to use the applications specialist because they had the skills to do it on their own. They sound to themselves like a selfless hero; they are in fact going against the agreed plan.

## Configuration & Quoting

So, we all know you cannot just buy a new car anymore - it needs configuration. Maybe Henry Ford had it right when he said, "they can have it any colour they want as long as its black."

Of course, the complexity of configuration depends on what you're selling and how it is purchased. Sometimes you have a simple price-list - things that can work together but don't necessarily have to. This is easy and tends to work for lower priced products.

Often, as companies grow, they look at product expansion to increase average sales price or fight off competitors. This is normally done by offering customisation, extensions, add-ons, and quality variations.

One industry that I have worked on the edge of was life science microscopy. The customer believes they are getting one of 6 defined models on the website when in fact they are building their burger around the bun.

Like a car, the answer to "how much is it?" depends on the items selected. In some cases, there are accessories and add-ons but most of the time a decision is needed for nearly every part.

The salesperson's job is to configure the solution for you - they are acting as a consultant based on identified and developed needs.

For companies with such products, they promote the capability of their core product - they don't promote the complexity and they fight to keep this under control. The art of configuration has been improved from having to learn the product portfolio (like a London taxi driver learning the streets), with the addition of configuration tools that make life easier, simplifying the job (like giving taxi drivers SatNav).

Over time, there are less configuration mistakes and the salespeople have been freed to work on other aspects of their game.

Anyone providing a solution which is customised, is going to have a more complex job in configuring; custom work means custom configuration - this is true for integrators and those selling services.

Configuration tools make life easier in situations like the microscope but there are fewer benefits if you are working on a large project such as a one-time custom solution.

The configuration completes the offering to the prospect; it is the end result of conversations where needs were explained and options selected, sometimes directly by the prospect and sometimes by the salesperson through their experience and judgement of the situation. The final part of this is the quotation. Often when you think you are done you may need to complete tender documents required under a bid process.

I'm amazed when people talk about taking 30 minutes to do quotes – I could do a quote from the CRM in 60 seconds. But for some there are multiple parts and multiple considerations. Even taking this into account, creating a quote should be possible for the salesperson to do incredibly quickly – this is easily achieved and controllable.

Quoting a piece of consultancy work is easy. As an example, if I believe it will require 20 days, the quote is day-rate x 20 – the quote pops out formatted in moments. The proposal however takes me one to two days to get right, explaining the why and why for you and ensuring expectations are correct etc.

Can I outsource this to another person? No, it's not worth it. I own the proposal.

What about the quote? Well, if it's not complex do it yourself. If it is maybe the salesperson should own it anyway. Some customers just need pricing to hand to their purchasing team; this can be provided by internal sales. However, in most instances quoting lives with the person who owns the suggested solution, the salesperson. You, as the leader, own the quote-making process or at least can have input into how it is generated. You need to make sure this is as easy as possible for the salesperson; for them it's a low-value, high-need job they must complete to progress the sale.

What if I had to complete a tender – could someone else help? Well here yes, I could push this out to other resources away from sales.

In one company I worked for we had salespeople across the globe all selling $50,000 to $250,000 products, they were experts in all areas of the KNOWLEDGE segment. I estimate they spent about 20-40% of their time working purchasing, proposals, quotes, tenders, etc. Here you could argue that a person responsible for the tendering could have saved the salespeople time. They would, I'm sure, argue that a tender for Stanford is too different to Argonne National Labs. I disagree but would agree that a Japanese or French tender may be very different.

Understandably salespeople will of course argue against most change until that change is proven to benefit them. They will defend aspects of their jobs that they absolutely hate in order to maintain control. Any change to a current situation must be very carefully considered and explained to the salesperson. Of course, you are in charge but that doesn't mean you get to force change without explaining how you made the decision and, having a discussion about the change.

*Demonstrating Capability*

I really like the term Demonstrating Capability which is a term unashamedly taken from SPIN Selling by Neil Rackham. For my first 10 years I always assumed that there had to be a demonstration in person, anything else would not work especially as all my competitors were demonstrating similar products in the same way. I also knew if I could get a demo in front of a customer I could win.
Demonstration of capability is a much better way of thinking about it. In its simplest form: prove to me that what you are offering me works and that I will be able to work it.
As I write, I have just purchased a golf net for my 11-year-old nephew for his birthday. No demo. Why? People assume it was the price, why would they demonstrate it, well I'm sure a golf store would have a much more expensive top of the range model that they would unpack and explain for me, but I chose the internet. Was that it? No.
The company who made it completed a large chunk of the demonstration of capability in the material, text, images, assembly video, etc. The rest was completed by the reviews of customers telling me it was good. My decision was comfortable because the capability was demonstrated, just not through a demonstration.
People buy when they are comfortable; some unease will of course be inevitable, but everyone has a limit of comfort needed to pull the trigger and buy. Creating comfort is a key job for the salesperson.
When we think of amazing salespeople, those that can sell ice to the Inuit people of Alaska, amazing hair, fantastic suits, charm personified – those ones, they are the masters in creating comfort.
Demonstration of capability as per my golf net example can be done in many ways. It's not that some products don't need a demonstration, it's that they don't need a demonstration to demonstrate capability.

I'm in a shop/store and I'm hungry and I see a Mars bar (for Americans that's a Milky Way). An American Milky Way is a British Mars bar, a British Milky Way is a Musketeer – I think it is very important to clear that up. Anyway, I see the chocolate bar and select it, no demo was done. However, there was some form of demonstration of capability for my brain to accept it. For example, they are allowed to sell it, so it's ok to eat, tick - it is capable. I've seen an advert on TV, the people seemed to be enjoying it, tick - it is capable, I have had chocolate before, I liked it, tick - it is capable.

So don't always rush to get in a car, plane, train to go and demonstrate the product live.

Some alternatives include:

- Brand trust
- Web written collateral
- Featured articles
- Reviews & references
- KOL recommendation
- Videos of product use
- Specifications
- Product trials
- Sale or return
- Acceptance testing
- Proposal / pitch
- Discussion
- Demonstration by web

In a past role our salespeople would occasionally sell a highly expensive camera to be used for physics research at synchrotrons, think CERN's Giant Hadron Collider and you would be nearly right. These were >$250,000 and each one had a different sensor variation, coating, mounting, etc. We never sold the same product twice - every customer was a little different. The number of variations was too large to ever create a situation where we could demo what the customer wanted.

The demonstration of capability was achieved through brand trust, collateral, specifications, and discussion.

Try-&-buy was another demonstration capability we adopted for our sub $20,000 products. Prospects still wanted to see the product, but the economics meant we could never travel or attend.

This was a concern - when you demonstrate the product, you are driving; you show how it works, you know all the buttons, it looks easy but now you're handing the responsibility over to an end-user to drive. For success, your product must ship well, work well, and have easy to follow support material. Taking what your salespeople sell today and shipping it to an end-user to try rarely works, you must make changes and develop your out-of-box experience making it as simple as possible.

With any loan of a product, physical or software, you must remember that you control how the loan or trial works; you can set up the experience and even speedbumps to encourage useful communication. You don't have to just let them get on with it.

As an example. "Your trial starts at 9am on Tuesday. During the set-up and activation call, we explain how the software works and the salesperson will obtain and activate your trial software licence."

The process explained seems fair to all involved. You are allowing them a free trial; in return you are giving (insisting on) some basic training, helping them assess the software correctly, eliminating frustrations, saving them time. Yes, they give up some control, and they may not get it 100% as they want, but it is all for their, and your, benefit.

You are free to add speedbumps to your sale or demo process to help increase hit-rate; if they are fair and add value for both parties, then they will appear reasonable to both parties.

I've found the best way is to not allow options or possible variation, replacing "We could do training?" with the stronger expectation setting statement "Then we do the training." Owning your process and making it repeatable makes your sales process scalable.

How you demonstrate capability can set you aside as novel business and give you a position. It can also act as a protective barrier. When we decided to go 100% try-&-buy for our entry-level products, we changed the website and put this new model at its heart; all the messaging was about how easy it was to evaluate our products.

We could get you a product to try within 3 days, we had all the tools online, it was super easy to understand, and we were set up to work this way. Others could imitate the loan but not the process and the fact that we staked claim to the position. We owned try-&-buy in that space.

We positioned ourselves as fast-to-try and fast-to-buy, we positioned our competitors as slow, in the dark ages or unprepared. We used the position to fight against the embedded market expectation which we viewed as old. We had our doubts - what if people rejected this new way of trying the products? In the end, it was fine. Our hit-rate which we were also concerned about falling, actually increased which drove up revenue. What had started as an efficiency play ended up being much more.

*Real World Demonstrations*

Salespeople love a demo, a day out with a customer showing off your product. When it works, your salespeople are kings or queens of sales, the product master, the audience is eating out of their hands. My colleague Tim used to refer to his job as driving up and down the country in a car he didn't pay for telling people he was clever. Tim got to play the magician over and over again with products he knew how to "make sing."

When it goes bad, it goes bad; like a stand-up failing, it goes flat. The prospect's time is wasted, and they remember your business for all the wrong reasons.

Depending on what you're selling, a demonstration can be 30 minutes or a few days, leaving the product with a customer afterwards is not a demonstration. It's a trial you've agreed after the demonstration.

A demonstration is either you showing your solution or having a customer try your solution with you there to help if they get lost. Your aim is to show them what their life would look like if they purchased your product. Imagine looking at a nice jacket in a store, putting it on and looking in the mirror. You are not thinking well this is practical you're thinking more about acceptance and looking, what us Gen X people refer to as, cool.

What demonstrations should not be is what my friend and long-term colleague, Matt, would call a voyage of discovery. A demonstration is a pre-planned executed play designed to demonstrate capability, it's not training, it is not explaining unconnected features – it's a focused effort to convince the prospect to buy.

Salespeople should walk in with relevant experience, open and ready to discuss, but what they can't do is work out if it's a solution together with the prospect. They should have established it as the solution upfront – that was the qualification of needs part of the initial discussions. The salesperson is now here to prove their recommended solution is correct.

Demonstrations are about control. From the moment your salesperson arrives people want to distract them and take over, they are excited and want to press every button your product has.

They want to test it (by which I mean try and break it), they want to get on, not listen to sales points. They want to fire questions; they want to try a completely irrelevant thing that has nothing to do with their needs. Brian is in, he is an expert as he did a course on this 10 years ago and wants to destroy your salesperson and reinforce his position as the alpha male.

As the demonstration starts something is not right – your team try and fix it. People are breathing heavily in annoyance like they paid for a show, but the actors are late on stage. Some lose interest, some disappear, others stare at phones or chat about the weekend.

Your team try their best to get it back on track but in the end, the prospect can't even remember your salesperson's name or that of your company, but they remember it didn't work and your salespeople were a bit "all over the shop."

It all goes wrong without your control, (if you're in control it may still go wrong, but usually because of factors you can't influence.)

Why does it go wrong? Because expectations are not set. People follow expectations.

Here is an example of how we used to set expectations: "This is basically how my company provides a worthwhile demo; I will arrive with the equipment, and I will then set up the equipment which will take about 30 minutes just to make sure it's all working. We can grab a quick coffee and then interested users and decision-makers can enter. I start with an introduction to me and the company, which is less than 3 minutes, talk about the product, show it quickly using example data/sample covering the basics and showing the X, Y, Z we discussed by phone, all of which should be 30-45 minutes. Following this you can pilot, and we can do whatever is needed until the demo ends. Does this work for you Mr/Mrs Customer?"

Even when doing a demo, salespeople should always confirm the steps to be covered, writing them on a large sheet of paper to be crossed off as completed; this helps the prospect know where they are and what more is to come. At no point should people be thinking "how long is this going to take?"

In markets where competition exists but no one has an overwhelming advantage, I find that the reasons demonstrations work are that they sell all the aspects of what people buy. In my experience people buy 30% because they like and trust the salesperson, 30% because they trust and align to the company/brand, 30% because of the product (of course it must do the job) and 10% on the price. Everyone usually focuses on the product and price which is a mistake. Salespeople must remember to sell themselves, why they are good enough to be there, and also to sell the company and why the buyer needs to partner with them.

Figure 4.2 - Reasons people buy

*Web Demonstrations*

Can you see my first slide? Web demos have come a long way. Software sales have been able to adopt this for a while as the screen you're viewing the meeting on is the one where you will probably view the software once purchased, so it's hardly a leap of imagination. Products, real 3d products are harder, possible yes, but not in the same way. Why do I know this? Well because the shopping channel exists. Here you can purchase jewellery or a cement mixer. See the way they touch and use the items, tell stories of benefits that match needs of personas or draw similarities to their own lives. Chances are you will need multiple cameras to get the point across, maybe even screen-in-screen to show software controlling the product along with the product moving, bleeping, or just looking awesome while backlit as if it were an item of design beauty.

I challenge everyone to get more involved in building web-demos into their sales, even if it's just a good steppingstone on the journey to the ultimate decision-making demo.

*Deal Making & Closing*

When I started running our dealer network across Europe, I decided to go on a mission to meet the dealers and their customers and to understand a little more. What I was met with was this one sentence. "It's different here James, everyone wants a discount."

This was not a revelation, people like a discount everywhere. From the early days of our existence people have been trading, trying to get the best deal. It's probably more that everyone wants a deal rather than everyone wants a discount.

This is only true where it is perceived that you can get a discount. Try walking into an apple store and asking for a discount! They may have a deal, but not a discount. Some markets have discount expectations that have been formed over time but, as the profit margins of the main players indicate, that discount has achieved nothing since everyone has accounted for this in the list price. It is therefore a waste of everyone's time as we dance for purchasing.

Because of the way purchasing teams operate we may need some management or experience involved in the discount negotiations. My school friend, Martin, once told me a very wise thing: never be the first to offer the discount because you lose power if you do. For example, if someone says "what discount can I get?" don't say a number because that is their new minimal expectation. If you say 10%, they now know 10% is normal so will want more. If they say 10% and you say that you heard of a deal, several years ago about twenty times larger than this one where the discount was 10%, but it required loads of meetings with loads of managers, then you're saying it's possible but a lot more work for them, and maybe they come back to 5%.

It's better to say: "You tell me what you think you need and why you think we got our price wrong?" Just remember that if purchasing dept. is negotiating, it's because they've been instructed to buy.

Discounting may be needed in situations where your price-to-value calculation is wrong or doesn't function in your particular market. We would regularly see a competitor sell a product for $20,000 in the USA but only $15,000 in France; importation and exchange rate headroom was the excuse but the reality was that they could achieve a higher price in America. Your company now has a choice: do you allow the team locally to discount more to counter this or do you set a more comparable price for France? I strongly recommend setting price so as not to alienate your sales team. By this I mean don't put your salespeople in a situation where they need to discount 25% to win. You're not giving the customer a discount of 25%; instead you're telling them that you were prepared to overcharge them by 25% if unchallenged.

Deals can help people to feel comfortable. However, it is too often offered before it's requested. Rarely do salespeople say "look, I don't get it, why have you not placed the order?" Instead, they start throwing discounts or ideas like free warranty. This devalues your product and price may have never been the reason for their lack of action. When the customer is asking for discounts, they have usually already purchased in their mind and now we can start the silly purchasing dance.

Deals can of course be promoted. Prospects with no particular issue, in the early stages, or on the edge, can be nudged over with a time-limited deal. Buy now and get a free ....... Promotions such as these should ideally come from product management working in tandem with the sales team.

Many years ago, I awoke to a series of emails from dealers annoyed about a bundle promotion that had been added to our website overnight. Neither I, nor any of my European team knew anything about it. I had to wait until 5:00 pm to speak to my manager in our West Coast headquarters, where I was told that the promotion was designed to fight a competitor in the USA. I was told not to worry - it was strictly for America - it was not going to be a problem. I asked him to tell me what the first "w" stood for in www!

Promotions need to be discussed with your team in the first instance in order to sort out potential problems earlier rather than later. Also, always remember that proper promotions take time to travel through your salespeople or other channels to the customer.

The alternative is to use a closing promotion. These are nice, fast, and designed to push people over the line. The classic example is car mats; any mainstream car company salesperson has authority to throw in the car mats - sometimes it is enough to get you to close on a deal based on a shortened timeline. Buy it today and I will throw in.......

The best deals I feel are done when the salesperson exploits a pain-point in the purchasing decision - a doubt or an objection. These are the ones which I believe are valid and useful, as they address the desire for comfort, and, as noted previously, when comfort hits the correct level for them, they can purchase.

I believe it was the UK Businessman Theo Paphitis who said, "good deals are done when both parties walk away with a balloon." This means both parties must win; the business is not winning just by getting the deal - they also need a balloon. Getting deals without balloons means you are more probably in survival mode rather than playing the market.

Many things can be traded with the customer to get a better deal or price - reference stories, payment speed, anything. Just never give a deal or discount without a positive beyond simply getting the order.

Who does this decision sit with? Internal sales, salesperson, sales manager, business owner/leader?

Most companies set up discount-authority rules. For example, entry level salespeople get 2% without approval, the next level up can get 5%, etc. - whatever works for you. Just make sure people don't discount just because they can - it destroys value.

I've always considered a discount pot - an allowance for salespeople to give away in discounts, where they keep a percentage of what's left at the end of the year. The alternative is paying on margin, this is always a hard one as salespeople knowing the products' COGS (cost of goods sold) is never a good idea. You could pay on a presumed margin which is simply a made-up margin rate. For example, the presumed margin is 30% and you get 10% of the presumed margin remaining after you discount. If you want to discount, you feel the pain as much as the business does. This is a better way of controlling margins than a pure revenue-based commission plan.

Let's consider a $100,000 sale, assume we pay a rep 3% commission so they get $3000 from this sale. If they give a 5% discount the company now gets $95,000 and the salesperson $2850. The salesperson lost $150 and the company lost $5000.

Now let's consider paying 10% commission on a presumed margin of 30%. The sale has a $30,000 margin pot so if no discount is given the salesperson gets $3000 of commission. If they discount by $5,000, the margin is now $25,000 and so the salesperson makes only $2500 on the sale, losing $500 in commission. I had a scheme like this many years ago, not only did I not discount as much, I added on services which I knew had higher margins like training and warranty because I could make more. Critically it makes the salesperson think about the money added to the business (margin) not just the revenue.

Whatever you choose you will want some control at management level as you don't want to create confusion. One region's discount may cause issues for another, especially where, as we will explain in the chapter on markets, multiple territories can make up a single communicative market.

Discounts are not bad but I prefer deals. Always judge the need relative to your need as a leader. Review the situation calmly. Just remember that they are tactics that you can choose to use or not.

As a leader, what you want to care about is product value and product margin based on average selling price, not on single deals. Single deals can afford to be tactical but, if you observe the margin being 40% when it was planned to be 60%, then you have a real problem.

On the other hand, deals can help enhance value especially (as noted) if you target concerns. I would always try to educate my sales leaders to understand what was possible and have them come to me to discuss; I owned the authority; understood the margins and impact, and they owned the ideas.

Discounts and deal-making need thought. Are they important for your business? Do they need controls? Who is responsible?

Next up is closing. Closing is an art form and, just as asking someone out on a date, it's often a problem of simply asking. However, the more confident you are of receiving yes as the answer, the happier you are to ask. This is why it was always considered easy by my highly attractive friends - for them the chance of yes was higher than for myself!

For simple transactional component sales this should be simple; for example, if you phone an airline and ask the price of a flight from London to Newark, they will tell you the price and ask if you want to pay Visa, Mastercard or American Express.

In solution sales, salespeople should operate in the same way if they are satisfied that the constituents of the sale have been completed and it is an appropriate time. If the customer says, "I would like a demo" and they are seeing competitors next week, don't say "would you like to place an order?" because this simply won't work - it's a beat out-of-time.

This is one of the reasons I like the STRONGMAN© Sales Process by Ed Wal. It helps me assess the sale and get to the point where I feel that I can ask for the order.

Part of closing is about personal empathy. Your salesperson is human, they have been honest about being a salesperson all along - it even says so on their email sign off and business card. "Dear Mr or Mrs Customer, I think we have everything sorted, I've answered all your questions and clearly you know that my job is to collect orders or I don't get paid. If you're happy with the solution, which you appear to be, please can you place the order?"

Personally, I love this alternative close "Do you want the red one or the green one?!"

Who closes is not about the time they've spent in the negotiation or deal - it's about authority and empathy. You may choose that for your business, salespeople can close the deal directly; some who use applications or new sales staff may want to have a regional manager more involved in closing, especially if there are concerns. Some may even want to dress up the close as a final meeting, with more key staff involved to lay out the project as they see it, and the next steps of implementation; it's a nice way to run an assumed close.

What some of you will find a little amazing is some salespeople don't actually close deals, by which I mean they win deals, they just don't intentionally close them by asking for the order. Many will just keep communicating with the prospect and keep waiting for them to offer the close, sometimes they just wait until they get an order.

| TACTICAL SUMMARY | |
| --- | --- |
| Listening & Positioning | Salespeople / Applications or Product Specialist / DE-EMPATHISE |
| Configuring & Quoting | Salespeople/ Administration/ Product Specialist / Configuration tools DE-EMPATHISE |
| Demonstrating Capability | Salespeople / Application Specialist/ Product Specialist / Collateral / DE-EMPATHISE |
| Deal Making | Salesperson/ Sales Director /Senior Management/Product Management |

## CHAPTER SUMMARY

The subsegments of DEVELOP are understanding needs, configure & quoting, demonstrating capability and deal making & closing.

The needs may need to be developed through prospect questioning or they may be obvious to all involved. If the salesperson does not understand the needs, there is a high chance that they don't understand the opportunity resulting ultimately in a lower hit-rate.

Needs within a sale can be categorised as application, business and personal. Salespeople and prospects are obsessed by understanding and selling to application needs.

Depending on the complexity of the needs and the breadth of your product portfolio you may need multiple people to understand the needs.

Some solutions are multicomponent and require a high degree of configuration. If it is complex your business needs to account for this time on the SalesDISK©.

Quoting should be made as simple as possible for salespeople. It is a required step but a low value one for the salesperson. For some there are the added complications of required written proposals and tender processes to contend with. Your business needs to account for this time on the SalesDISK© or find a way to support it.

Demonstrating capability can be done in numerous ways, many of which are to be used in combination. Salespeople or product/applications specialists will feature heavily in any product demonstrations carried out in person or via the web.

Product demonstrations are best when they are executed plays where you remain in control, versus a voyage of discovery often required due to poor understanding of needs.

Deal making and discounting are tactics. They need controlling but can be used with good effect when needed. Your business needs to identify the types of deals used, who is to create them and how they are deployed.

Deal making during the close of a sale is a common tactic requiring a highly intimate understanding of the situation from the sales team. This can be established using techniques such as STONGMAN© developed by Ed Wal.

# Chapter 5: IDENTIFY

DEVELOP was about progressing, convincing and winning opportunities, IDENTIFY, as the name would suggest is about finding them. Some of you may be thinking this is a section on marketing, sadly not as noted as SalesDISK© is always presented from the Salesperson's point of view.

| SEGMENT | SUBSEGMENT | DEFINITION |
|---------|------------|------------|
| IDENTIFY | Lead Processing | Responding to inbound requests for discussion, information, and pricing |
| | Farming | Outbound contact of existing customers in search of new business opportunities |
| | Prospecting | Outbound contact of new prospects with the intention of discovering or developing a need |
| | Business Development | Focused effort in finding new areas of business. Examples being investigating new markets, finding alternative uses for products, channel development and expansion, etc |

Figure 5.1 – Subsegments & definitions

The key questions we have to answer are:

- Where do opportunities come from?
- How much responsibility do sales have in finding new business?
- How do marketing leads get processed?
- What is business development and who should do it?

Marketing of course does lead generation in all forms. I say all forms because many people believe that only actions which result in completed contact web-forms are lead generation. That's not true - lead generation is every activity carried out by marketing when communicating with prospects and existing customers.

Opportunities come from many sources - leads are simply one of those sources, others are found by salespeople through their own efforts. Any activity where a customer contacts your business or salesperson directly, can be considered to be a marketing lead. The salesperson's job here is to respond to the lead to create an opportunity, and so service the demand. Any opportunity created when a salesperson contacts a prospect through a means of interruption, is a sales-generated opportunity.

How many of your projects are as a result of marketing leads or sales-generated opportunities?

In my experience creating a solid link between marketing leads and opportunity creation can be quite hard. In my past, I have built reports and dashboards to model this and at best we could identify about 30% of business recorded as coming from marketing leads.

There were a few reasons for this:

1. Record keeping. People just don't record the lead/opportunity source correctly.
2. Definition. If a customer calls your salesperson and wants another unit, this is marketing generated as they created the product and all that goes with it. You could argue that it was not created by marketing communication (who may have created the first sale), but it was not created by the salesperson either - they simply serviced it.

3. Channels. Customers like OEM's and dealer channels often get left out, marketing clearly played a part in the product, and marketing communication may have created the initial lead. Even if sales created the lead through prospecting, surely marketing communication played a part, if only in branding so that customers recognise the company name.

This is important to point out as salespeople often see marketing as simply activity (email, tradeshows, adverts, web development, etc) and response (web forms). They forget all the additional things that marketing do. Marketing is always doing lead generation but not necessarily in a way obvious to salespeople.

In the last chapter I told you about my interview and review question: Rank these 4 parts of the sale from most favourite to least favourite, find, first key interaction, demo, close.

Everyone, and I mean everyone, I worked with put find last. It is the hardest part and of course salespeople just want to knock deals into the back of the net. "If you put 5 demos in front of me a week, I will give you 3 to 4 orders, why do I need to waste my time finding them, surely that's marketing."

I've noted several times now the need for sales and marketing leaders to be aligned. One of the reasons is that single line that gets spouted from every salespersons mouth at some point: "Why can't marketing just give me more leads."

For some salespeople, marketing will produce enough leads for salespeople to service them. Let's assume we have these magical contact forms that get completed online and arrive simultaneously in your salesperson's inbox and CRM. Who is going to deal with them? How are you going to deal with them?

*Lead Quality*

The first point is the ease of dissecting quality – how much cleaning do they need and are they really leads? I'm going to start with an experience of poor lead quality. Many years ago, part of my responsibilities within the group was to run a European sales operation for a software company. The software did 2 jobs – it controlled various external components and it analysed images. We had a dealer network across Europe, and we had a team selling directly in the UK.

The only way for anyone to make money on these products was to dress them up and sell them as systems or solutions. The software sold on average for $5000, dealers got on average discount of 30% or $1,500 so this was not enough margin when you considered the time to discuss, demo, install, train and support. Increasing the ASP by adding hardware could bring this up to $15,000-$50,000 making it become a worthwhile proposal.

And here was the problem; the dealer network controlled the integration solutions and the software company wanted to sell software, so all the lead generation tactics were focused on the unattractive analysis solutions - so what did we get? We got leads for software that we couldn't sell economically to achieve our goals, and we got loads of them.

What was worse was that the price of the product prohibited most prospects from ever purchasing, so it was a double miss. In the end, it was more efficient not to service the leads, which sounds crazy, but we made more money by ignoring them and getting on with prospecting for integration solutions. We, of course, responded with an automated email and tried to take them through a process, but it was designed to filter through to the best opportunities. Today, in a world of licence protected trials, online demos, and various content mediums, this would have been an internet sale.

When a salesperson sits down to contact a lead, you want them to be thinking this is going to be another winner - not this will be a waste of my time. Bad leads don't just come in the form of quality misses - they can also be contacts who are not at the right stage for advancing, research-not-review or simply not a lead. Are you screening leads before they get to salespeople?

Who is responding to the lead and how competent do they need to be?

Yesterday, I heard a story of a salesperson targeted with selling >$100,000 instruments getting chewed and spat out by the company president because he didn't respond within 24 hours to a lead for a $3000 accessory. Clearly the buyer needs to be answered but you want the right people on the right things; internal sales or even service would have handled the request better.

Does your buyer want hard-core information and to talk to experienced staff instantly? Will they be irritated by an internal salesperson since now they have to explain their questions twice? This is for you to decide based on your buyers and the information you think they are searching for.

How are you asking customers to communicate with you? Phone, contact forms, email, live chat?

Contact forms, in combination with autofill functions in web browsers, are now easy to complete and are commonplace. Without forms my lead volume would look terrible but my conversion rate would be immense - why? Salespeople only enter good leads into the CRM. You can't blame salespeople - in fact a leader needs to protect the salespeople from unnecessary admin and maximise the time available to do their job. Using forms which feed directly into the CRM helps salespeople save time and helps you understand the real quality of the leads being generated.

When I was a salesperson my number one mission was to get a lead on the phone. I knew that if I could get them on the phone, I had a chance. However, some buyers don't want the phone, or maybe they don't want the phone yet. We live in an email-happy world - that is fine, sometimes it's enough, just understand that meaningful transactions occur more often when there is a good free-flowing dialogue. If possible, use email to get them on the phone.

*Leads that are not Leads*

If you've never done sales then you won't understand this, but every so often a manager will send an email to the salesperson with a name, email, phone number or possibly a weblink to a company page or a LinkedIn profile - nothing more, no reason, no explanation. This is not a lead - this is audience identification. I'm not saying they might not buy something but it's not a lead. If you want to give me a list with a message and a mission then maybe I'm with you.

Other sources of audience identification which people mix up as leads are webinar sign-ups - yes they are interested but they never said "contact me", they are really in a marketing funnel. However, as far as management is concerned why not call them, you have time?

Next is anyone contacting the company for service - you might want to say hello? Or a person at a trade show taking a pen and getting their badge scanned, or a purchased list of people who attended an event or trade show? I feel that I'm going to explode at this point – these people are audiences, simply people whose name and addresses we have obtained, they are not leads, I have a database full of people like this thank you. Some of them may even be "in research" but they are very rarely "in review" (these are the ones that fill in "Contact us" forms with questions).

Why not call them anyway? Stop! If you have not done sales you don't understand. The job is to hit quota – sometimes monthly, sometimes quarterly and sometimes yearly, whilst being judged constantly on a graph of bookings and revenue.

Salespeople spend their time with two clear buckets of jobs – leads and opportunities. The opportunities are those that can become orders, leads are the ones which can become opportunities. To get to quota you need to keep emptying the opportunities bucket (orders) and refilling it from the leads bucket.

Salespeople are simple beings – empty the buckets; sell to every opportunity; call the leads list and qualify them in or qualify them out. The more efficient you can make this system, the better they will be at selling consistently. Just remember that they have simply two buckets. Everything else you give them to do will break this cycle and will be a distraction, even if it's one they enjoy,

The other key thing I mentioned was that leads get qualified in or qualified out. Salespeople are looking for business that is going to convert to sales relatively quickly, so although some projects will convert from research to review, the salespeople will close the leads in CRM because they fall between buckets. Salespeople can nurture old leads but again, it's a matter of efficiency.

So why call audiences unless you need to top up a bucket? It takes more time to convince a prospect the further they are from consideration. If the opportunity bucket looks empty, what do you do? Well, you look in the leads bucket, what if the leads bucket is empty well then you call the audiences, you farm and you prospect.

If the buckets are not empty and you start asking for such things, you will break the bucket cycle (and no one likes broken buckets, just ask dear Liza!).

So why do leaders/managers make these comments, send these emails, and get so annoyed about leads? Well firstly, they feel like they've paid for them; secondly the further you are from a lead the better it looks. Every lead looks good to a manager.

We once had a tick option on the web contact form that simply said, "interested in multiple-unit pricing." Some people ticked it and when questioned they all said, "it depends on how much it is" - of course it does. After getting the lead you might get another email from the manager (to handle outside your bucket cycle) saying "this a great lead, did you call them yet?"

What if the bucket system keeps everyone busy and you need more? Well simple - look for efficiencies in the bucket system. Could an internal salesperson prequalify the leads?

There is even a specific title given to these people who take this task on, they are called SDR's sales development reps. Their job it to take inbound leads and set up meetings with more qualified salespeople.

This can work. Again, salespeople can get grumpy about adding people into their world and sometimes they would be right to do so.

One morning we got an email from the president telling us that from now on all leads in Europe and America would be pre-screened through a lady in our Canadian factory. No problem had been identified with lead-flow, no metrics were in place to say it was an issue, there was no consultation or review period, it was just an email. Sales were simply to hand over lead qualification to a part-time person working from the West Coast, who had no knowledge as we would define it in the KNOWLEDGE segment.

Three months, and several arguments later this was reversed. There had been no plan, no training, just action. Could it work? Of course, it could have worked and in fact many years later we covered entire product lines for the Americas using internal salespeople from the UK costing four times less than a field salesperson in America. This in turn freed up those American salespeople to work on higher value sales.

Doing it wasn't wrong - doing it badly was. It was a pure and simple example of misalignment and lack of sales strategy design.

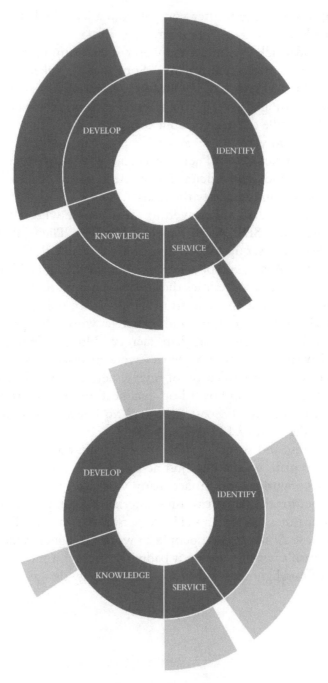

Figure 5.2 - shows the SalesDISK© - salespersons responsibility top, internal sales responsibility, bottom. www.salesdisk.com.

As noted in the last chapter implementing changes like these in existing sales teams can be hard. Salespeople will of course need to be heard, and it's fine and correct for them to be heard - they might be right. However, if you present them with diagnoses, options considered and a plan of how it's going to work, and they still want to argue, then they need to mentally move on, or quite literally move on.

If you think your salespeople will be fully occupied with DEVELOP or SERVICE then you should consider adding people to help with the IDENTIFY segment. Internal salespeople can do the additional work, calling audiences and dealing with new inquiries. It can be part of a role or, if volume allows, the entirety of their role.

When the leads bucket runs dry what do salespeople do? Some will slow, those experts in servicing leads simply explain it as a slow market. This used to drive me up the wall. For me there are times when it's frantic and times when it's busy, busy is the normal. Slow just indicates that they are only willing to (or capable of) servicing marketing leads. Christmas is slow, some people can argue that August is slow in France, but most of the time it's not slow, they have just emptied their buckets and rather than attempting to fix the situation they are saying "let's wait until the tap goes back on."

Another group will keep working the same buckets, just calling for updates, which are effectively just continuations - keeping busy achieving nothing but feeling like a good citizen. The final group will make every effort to find more prospects.

I believe the reality is that most salespeople that get to or exceed quota have good marketing leads but need some amount of top up from farming and prospecting. Of course, you can throw examples of the reverse in each direction, this is just an observation, and I used the word most - so don't bite!

The problem is that salespeople don't really like cold calling - we've all been interrupted and hated it. However, the dislike of the interruption is more about the value of the interruption and what it was interrupting. If you're interrupting a boring internal training on the use of corporate letterheads maybe you will jump at the chance to talk. If you're trying to leave for the day and have to get home before the traffic hits then it's "Go away."

If the interruption added value and helped, then it may be worthwhile. A classic field-based account manager tactic would be to call a list of existing CoolMatic4500 customers, introducing themselves and saying that they are going to be in the building on Thursday and can they stop by to say hello and check out the instrument. Sounds pretty reasonable, especially if you're an expert in Coolflip solutions. This is even more common amongst consumables salespeople - they're often arranging meetings to discuss needs and alter volumes for existing orders.

The worst interruption is a low value advert, "I'm calling today to tell you about how CoolMatic5000 is going to change your world."

Even the most resilient anti-prospecting salespeople will at least attempt farming by arranging to visit existing customers when they are in a region - why? They like them, they've built a working relationship, and they know that if they can develop a need, maybe they can sell something.

Other than interrupting, salespeople don't want to invoke a list of questions and minor issues that may lead to a loss of time – "they didn't want to buy anything, but I spent 30 minutes talking them through this mode of operation."

The biggest reason salespeople don't like to call is the fact that it's most likely a second or repeat call. The second call is the hardest call unless there is a solid reason to have it. I remember Eddie of STRONGMAN© fame once telling me of clients of his in America who would fire salespeople for starting calls with "I'm just calling to see how it's going". No - you're not - that is a lie. Every time your salesperson dials, they need purpose and need a measurable outcome.

So, if the second call is really hard, why is the first call easy? Because it's an introduction to a person who may be useful to them. "Hello, my name is Dave, I work for CoolMatic Instruments, and we are a market leader in Coolflip technology in which I know you're involved. I'm calling to introduce myself and see how you're using Coolflip technology and to see if I can help."

People are nice, they may even let salespeople present, show their stuff. It's a relatively low-cost investment in time for them - sometimes the salesperson has to travel across a country, while the prospect just needs to walk downstairs to collect them from reception.

People are also on the lookout for new technology. This is true if you're a tech-led end-user or OEM considering new products to build for their customers. What is happening in the first call is reversing a trade show booth conversation. Instead of them walking up to your booth, your salesperson is calling them.

The second call is sort of the annoying continual walking past each other at the trade show after the first exchange - you nod and say "got to stop meeting like this." You don't have anything to say, that is why the second call is so hard and that is why salespeople don't like it.

Salespeople are eager to call if you can present them with a solid reason to - a visit to their area, a new product which they know would help them, a webinar you want them to attend, etc - they just need leading to water with a call to action.

Beyond farming is prospecting; there is less connection to these contacts and so the salesperson has less authority to interrupt them. The connection is, at best, just a presumed need based on their segmentation. This is of course significantly harder for your salesperson.

Some salespeople live by prospecting. For them, IDENTIFY is greater than 50% of the job, but for others it's considered top-up, a bucket re-fill and to be deployed in a worst-case scenario.

For pure lead-generation, I have found that outsourced direct-marketing companies or internal salespeople can do it really well; they are less hung up on all the mental barriers and defences that get in the way of salespeople, including the bucket system.

*Leading the Horse to Water*

If you want to interrupt the bucket system and overfill your leads and opportunities buckets, then you need to find a way to fit this into the salesperson's world. This can be done in a couple of ways - installing it as a metric or adding focused time.

It is very easy for a salesperson to write 15 emails to new people each week. They can never use the excuse of people not answering the phone, so the minimum expectation is 15 outbound emails written with empathetic tone. If you have 15 emails sent a week you must be able to get a third of them on the phone, so 5 phone calls is a minimum expectation a week. If you get 5 phone calls then booking at least 2 web meetings must be possible. In total it sounds reasonable to ask for 15 outbound emails, 5 connections by phone and 2 meetings booked. This type of expectation-setting, if installed and correctly driven in a business, can see prospecting take hold. It is far better than "did you call that person whose details I sent you by email?". You could call it the 15:5:2 program, or whatever numbers or name you want. Just remember that this cannot be in combination with a dozen other non-bucket jobs you have given them.

The other method of driving farming and prospecting efficiency is by building dedicated time to do it, whilst you press pause on the bucket system.

Our direct sales business regularly suffered from low bucket syndrome – the pipeline was lacking and we needed to fix it. We would arrange dedicated calling events designed to force farming and prospecting calls.

These were also good team events and good opportunities for coaching – the concept was simple and not special. Salespeople are still free to run their buckets systems, but we are all going to meet for three days every four weeks to prospect.

A classic location for my US meetings was at the Marriott at Newark airport or at the one in Chicago (if you're familiar, it's the one connected to the Outback restaurant where blooming onions helped me put on weight!). The idea was that everyone could get there with just one flight, including me from the UK. We would hire a meeting room and would set up a schedule to cover all time zones. A series of contact lists would be provided so that people did not have to do any preparation – they just needed cell phones, pens, and paper.

| POSSIBLE CALLING LIST | REASON FOR CALL | TYPE |
|---|---|---|
| Customers Segmented by Products | Upgrade promotion | FARMING |
| Customers Segmented by Application | Need review, offer trial, push to webinar | FARMING |
| Customers Segmented by Region | Arrange visit during upcoming trip | FARMING |
| Dormant Leads | Re-investigate needs | FARMING |
| Dormant Opportunities | Re-investigate needs | FARMING |
| Close Lost Opportunities | Re-investigate needs | FARMING |
| Webinar Attendees | Introduction and need exploration – push to webinar | PROSPECTING |
| Trade Show Attendees | Introduction and need exploration – push to webinar | PROSPECTING |
| Scraped Application Based User Lists | Introduce. Investigate future needs, obtain permission for marketing | PROSPECTING |
| Scraped Competitor Based User Lists | Introduce. Investigate future needs, obtain permission for marketing | PROSPECTING |
| Targeted Account Contacts | Introduce. Investigate future needs, obtain permission for marketing | PROSPECTING |

Figure 5.3 - Example calling lists to be provided to salespeople for organised outbound calling sessions

Each list lived both on paper and in the CRM. If you logged a call against a contact, then the list would auto-update removing them, and you would not risk calling the same person twice. Every morning we would hand out new printed lists, with those contacted removed. Each list also had a call to action and reason to call. We would even print posters and put them around the meeting room so everyone could be aware of the reason or key promotions which might help whilst on the call.

The regional manager would keep score, logging the dial-outs, contacts made, and good results, including opportunities found. We also watched the prospected call numbers increase as the call lists reduced in size.

The rules were simple, just call - emails and notes can wait for the breaks. During any gaps deals could be discussed, coaching was happening and critically we would do something fun each day, the usual stuff like bowling or minigolf.

We would even run what we called the Ryder Cup where America and Europe competed in calling days with prizes. It was focused and it was metric - it worked for us.

I've seen other ways of doing this such as "new customer Tuesday", but all come down to the same thing – set aside time and help with the who-to-call and what-to-say.

To successfully help salespeople farm or prospect I recommend the following

1. Build it into their jobs and culture through expectations, either as time-based objectives or by taking dedicated time to focus on the activity
2. Measure it (what gets measured gets done)
3. Give them reasons to call, with outcomes and next actions to set. They can of course help in the creation of these actions, just don't rely on them to do so
4. Own the audience lists and if possible, make sure they come from the CRM, so that the communications and activities are recorded
5. Maintain consistency - don't let programs fade away. It's not "let's try" - it's "this has been researched, investigated, planned and we are now doing it this way."
6. Limit other interruptions and initiatives but let them have time to run their buckets

To be honest just be empathetic. Think of their objections and overcome them with planning and compromise. "If I were in their shoes, what would I want?" If you can't do this then either get help or give real thought to whether you want to be a sales leader or director. Empathy from sales management normally comes from experience of having done a similar job. I've worked with some people who have learnt sales from a book or by observation and it's interesting to watch. It for sure makes the job harder. I once watched a sales manager who had converted from another discipline tell their staff to "just call up the customer like this.....". It failed - they ignored them. They had never done it, never lived it and could not prove to the sales team that what they wanted would drive anything. Salespeople like to see your battle scars, which can be from different wars, but they want authentic authority. Who doesn't?

*Business Development*

Finally, let's look at business development which the art of making a business better. Ok, so everyone wants to make the business better and most people try every day. I've seen the term used in many places in business, sometimes in marketing and sometimes in sales.

For example, a business development manager is designated to grow the business by investing new routes to business, investigating new channels, new markets, and new relationships. Who would not want this? Often, it's a title given to a salesperson who has been given a job for which a quota cannot be assigned because no one quite knows what it will be. It can also sit really early in the process within marketing where people look for opportunities for which products should be designed.

To be great at business development I believe that you must have the skills and inquisitive nature of a marketeer mixed with the desire for drive and action of a salesperson. Having a quota is a distraction to this. Every so often people believe that they have a quota when in reality they have a payment mechanism. For example, product managers would have compensation systems linked to performance - this is a way to enable people to be paid and to encourage correct activity; this is not a quota. Quotas are counted once. If the business has a budget revenue of $10M and 10 salespeople with a quota of $1M of revenue each, that is the quota accounted for. If you want to pay sales managers, product managers, department heads on performance metrics to encourage good things, that's fine - they are just not quotas.

So, can salespeople do business development? For a hyper-busy direct salesperson, I would not see this deep-thought process be worthwhile, the needs are too far away from their regular conversations, and you are distracting their bucket work.

For people working in slower-paced sales jobs such as OEM sales or dealer channel management where a lot of the time they're thinking and investigating, I can see some possibility. Their bucket system is far less demanding and they can afford to take a week out to look at other things.

One thing I see a lot of is the confusion of prospecting with business development and I view the two things as very separate. If you are calling someone relating to an existing product, to be used for the purpose the product was intended for, with the desired outcome being a sale, you are prospecting; any other type of calling could be considered business development.

If the salesperson books a venue and holds a day of talks given by experts in their field to attracted targets, this is prospecting. However, if a salesperson calls a customer in an adjacent market to discuss whether their products may be relevant, this would be considered a business development activity.

What if a salesperson wants to improve their coverage and seeks to add another dealer? Well, this is simply channel development. Many businesses employ a dealer channel or distribution managers, but some have to run mixed models where a direct or end-user focused salesperson has to wear two differing skilled hats. In such circumstances you tend to use dealers to service low volumes or assist in complicated markets.

For the purposes of SalesDISK© I consider dealer channel development to be a subset of business development if it's an additional role, but if you're the channel manager then its just part of everyday work.

If the salesperson is responsible for searching out new OEMs, this is really just prospecting and part of everyday work.

Salespeople naturally get involved in business development due to their geographical location. For example, if you want to target a business in a new market in Germany, but are based in California, then you may choose to use your local salesperson on the ground to help.

As with prospecting, adding business development to a salesperson's role should be done with care. Making sure that time is being made for it and that expectations are set will be key to any success. Asking people to do business development without first explaining what it means to you, what it involves, what you want, and by when you need it, will result in nothing but frustration and confusion. Like all things that you ask a salesperson for, you need clarity and to deploy empathy.

| TACTICAL SUMMARY | |
| --- | --- |
| Lead Processing | Salespeople / Applications or Product Specialist / DE-EMPATHISE |
| Farming | Salespeople/ Internal Sales / Marketing / DE-EMPATHISE |
| Prospecting | Salespeople / CRM / Internal Sales /Marketing / DE- EMPATHISE |
| Business Development | Salespeople / Business Development Manager, Product Manager/ Marketing Manager/ EMPATHISE |

## CHAPTER SUMMARY

Lead-generation is every activity carried out by marketing when communicating with prospects and existing customers.

Marketing leads are the result of any activity where a customer contacts your business or salesperson directly.

Opportunities created when a salesperson contacts a prospect through a means of interruption, is a sales-generated opportunity.

Lists of names, organisations, phone numbers and emails organised into segments are audiences.

Salespeoples' main focus is to empty their opportunities bucket by getting orders, refilling it from the leads bucket. Any interruption needs to be handled carefully.

Internal salespeople, specifically sales development reps can be deployed to assist with screening and calling leads, selecting the best to move on to salespeople.

Most salespeople are going to be required to do some farming and prospecting to achieve quota.

Salespeople hate interrupting but you can help overcome this by providing them with solid reasons to interrupt, which provide value to the customer.

Farming is always easier than prospecting, as when farming you already have a confirmed shared interest and have a degree of authority to defend making the call.

If you want salespeople to farm and prospect, I recommend building this into their expectations and allowing or allocating them time to do it.

Business development and prospecting are often confused. Business development is more about taking steps beyond your current situation.

Business development is best done by people not distracted by quota obligations and who have time to investigate and research.

As with prospecting if you want people to do business development, you need to build it into expectations and be very clear of what is expected and how people are to go about it.

# Chapter 6: SERVICE

SERVICE relates to every activity involving the customer post-purchase. In a way, it is the customer journey, as opposed to the buyer journey, taking us from the minute the product is purchased to the end of its useful life.

| SEGMENT | SUBSEGMENT | DEFINITION |
|---|---|---|
| SERVICE | Installation & Training | Completing the commitments of the sale and ensuring that the product is used as intended |
| | Customer Support | Answering questions and helping customer throughout the life of the product |
| | Customer Engagement | Engaging with customers, ensuring their satisfaction, and obtaining references and referrals |
| | Warranty, Upgrades and Add-ons | Selling additional products and services to customer beyond that of the company's core offerings |

Figure 6.1 – Subsegments & definitions

SERVICE can be many things - it can be an obligation, a distraction, and an opportunity. Like all segments, there needs to be tight control over who is responsible for what internally. However, unlike the other segments there is an additional job to be done which is setting the expectations to your customers. If this is not clear, the misalignment will cause tremendous damage to your relationship with that customer and others they communicate with. Providing high or low service does not create bad relationships or create negative press, impacting future sales - it is the misalignment of expectations that does that.

Markets normally have pre-built expectations of service set over many years by their leading suppliers or customer demands. For example, on-site support or installations may be the norm. This does not mean it is required by your business or that the market standard cannot be redefined for your business. What it does mean is that if you're not going to meet the standards of the market, you had better make that clear and you'd better explain why. Did you do it to save customers money, make it faster, easier, or even greener?

So how much SERVICE are you going to require, who is going to do it and how are you going to communicate it?

The key questions for you to answer about your business are:

- What involvement of your business is required in the use of the product post-purchase?
- What expectations have you set based on the sale?
- What impact does the use of your product have on future purchases?
- Can post-sale activities be leveraged to drive more sales?

*Completing Commitments – Installation and Training*

I sometimes think that salespeople should be called purchase order people because that is the main mission for many of them - the sale is the declaration of revenue and by now many salespeople are long gone. Most salespeople are compensated on revenue recognition counted from when the product ships. In this way the salesperson is considered to be sharing in the risk in some way; some get paid on orders but very few in my experience.

So, to many salespeople, customers are ships passing in the night, we did a deal, no biggie, nice to meet you, I'm on to the next. For others we are on to the next phase of our relationship which may last for many years. This can be as a repeat supplier of products or in the case of a single solution, just until we prove it does exactly what we said it would when you purchased it.

For these single solutions (one-time buys) we need to complete the expectations set by the salesperson when positioning the product; this can include support, assistance, installation, and training. At this point I want to clarify my position on this - I hate post-sales activities being left floating in the sales model for salespeople to design, case by case.

Firstly, if you're providing an installation or training it should be clearly shown as a line item on the quotation. You do not have to charge for this service - that's up to you, your specific markets expectations and on which elements you choose to make your money. You simply need to show it on the quotation as an item to be completed. This helps your business to plan what it needs to deliver, and helps the prospect understand what they are getting and how they will start their journey with your products after purchase.

Secondly, what you plan on providing should be written down, this can be in a proposal or contract, or even better in a web or pdf document provided to all customers to set standards.

The more commitment required internally and externally for installation and training, the more time should be spent on productising them and ensuring that sales have adequate material to set the expectations pre-purchase. If little commitment is required for installation and training then do the minimum to meet, or define market standards e.g., web videos, quick start guides, etc.

In my very first year of selling, I sold a camera and software package for about $10,000 to a customer in Glasgow. At the time I promised that the next time I was in the area I would do the installation and training. Under some pressure I agreed that I would return in 3 weeks - sooner than I wanted to but I needed the order to hit my quota. I had already discounted to get the deal, but I just needed it closed so I agreed to terms I was unhappy with.

I arrived on a rainy Tuesday morning for my first appointment of the week having driven up the night before. I gave a pretty reasonable run-through and said, "excellent, that's me done, thanks for the business, let me know if you need any more." At this point the customer said "but that's just the first group - we have you booked for the next two days". I said, "I'm sorry, I've only allowed for half a day because it's a simple product." The customer's response was that when he purchased his $750,000 Confocal Microscope the training took all week – he was unamused when I asked him for a further $740,000.

This was a pure and simple expectation error. I should have sold the training and installation separately – I should have used not providing an installation as the reason to give the discount or I should have just walked away from the deal knowing it was not going to be worth it. However, when you're young, some bread is better than no loaf, by which I mean you suck at trading time for money, as you don't see or understand opportunity cost.

I never wanted to repeat this experience. If I was going to have to do installations to meet the market standards, they were going to be smooth, repeatable and something I sold. Everyone else in my market followed the "I will show you how it works next time I'm about" model so I documented the new install expectation and our sales team used it to sell against this poor, variable offering of ambiguity. Selling against ambiguity is easy, unwritten promises are simply that, just watch one episode of Judge Judy and witness it in every case.

We managed to sell installations at $500 for a half day and $800 for the day – quite a lot for 20 years ago. We then tackled training, we didn't want to spend time on customers site doing training, so we wrote a specific course and delivered it at a training facility near to our office. This cut down on our travel and allowed us to scale as we could train multiple customers in one session. We could even return to existing customers to sell them training, either as an expansion or to help get new staff up and running with our products. You could still have training onsite if you wished, but we made it disproportionately more expensive. We sold the new program as a polished, professional, and repeatable course to be completed in an environment where you could not be distracted by your day job – often the problem when training was conducted at a customer site. We charged $500 a day and ran the course every month. It was a service, it had value, we sold it as such. It also had a side benefit, it allowed us to build closer relationships with our customers and explore new possible projects.

The program was a success and within 12 months we employed a person to do the installations and run the training courses, all self-funded by the new revenue stream. Revenue was up, margins were up and critically the salespeople were now free to expand and focus on the IDENTIFY segment and get moving on growing the business, which we did.

Roll forward 10 years and I was selling a new product into a new market. The company I was working for had originally been the market leader but fell backwards to competitors over time due to lack of investment and focus. Part of the re-launch was focused on training, this time for free. We, the sales team, provided generic training and demonstrated how the technology worked using our products. Our pitch was simple, we will show you how to use the technology and get the best from it. It was intended to be educational, focused, and vendor agnostic. We could help you understand the technology even if you had our competitors' products. It was about the technology and getting the most from it, I'm not going to lie - flipping competitor's customers was however the net result and boy was it fun.

It helped us re-establish our position as a technical market leader and created customer intimacy. At the heart of it was the softest-of-touch message "do you want free training and dinner?". This helped drive farming and prospecting within the IDENTIFY segment. It was also heavily used to convert prospects in the DEVELOP segment "Unsure if it's us or our competitor? Well come on our course and let's talk about it."

A customer even asked one of my salespeople if they could send two more of their staff on the 'indoctrination' course. He knew, like us. this was the deal - we provide value, so we get to talk a little about us and our products. It's no different to the deal you do with YouTube - want to watch a free video, then watch 5 seconds of an advert before you can press skip. This intimacy paid off - we got invited to participate in more deals and won any active deal where the prospect attended the course. If you came on the course, chances were that you were going to end up buying from us at some point in the future.

The courses helped the team prospect - every salesperson is looking for a good reason to call customers and this was a winner. You may be thinking to yourself "You focused your salespeople on giving away a free course - are you mad?" Kind of yeah, but the reality was I focused them on pipeline building and closing open deals.

So, let's return to providing installations and training in your business - who is going to do it? Salespeople are often ok with providing installations as long as they have reasonable product knowledge, but they often need help with training because they confuse training with a longer demonstration. Sometimes they do the reverse - confusing the demonstration with product training, which is worse, both boring and confusing the prospect during the evaluation. In a similar vein, installation is not showing every feature (that is the manual) - it is about showing the user how to do the specific jobs they want to repeat.

Of course, some products don't need installation and training. In a world of start-up guides, YouTube videos and web meetings you can control a lot of what used to require the salesperson to travel for. Alternatively, dedicated staff can do installations and training or simply make this part of an application or product specialists role.

In my opinion salespeople who are busy running the bucket game should have no time for installation and training. If possible, I want this excuse removed, and it is an excuse I have heard too many times. No matter how many times I was thrown this excuse, I knew some salespeople loved being with customers and doing installations, it gave them an opportunity to learn more about the products and customers and possibly show off their knowledge. For some it was an excuse they could pull out of their back pockets when behind quota.

I completely understand the value some salespeople get from continuing a relationship beyond the order to installation and training, but there must be enough business that can be pulled out of this relationship in the short to mid-term for me to see it as real value – this is somewhere between 1 or 2 years.

Salespeople, like all people, will sometimes subconsciously self-sabotage their time by creating barriers entirely of their own making, building in very high standards for things which should be quite simple. For example, if they get to define the installation process, they may want it to be 5 days, each customer requiring custom PowerPoints, install guides, and freshly baked cakes. Again, this comes from ambiguity, if you have not set standards over how installations and training work, then be prepared for others to do so for you.

So, where do you draw the line? For me, if a salesperson needs to do five days of installs a month, then I would rather use another resource and free up five more salesperson days to use on the IDENTIFY segment. This is of course if I can occupy the installer on the other 16 working days with something of value. This can, be market or territory dependent – for one person to be flying across the USA for example could get tiring although it's not impossible and I've seen it done, but could a person in China cover Japan 5 days a month?

Scale makes decisions like this significantly easier; the problem goes away when the size of your business needs 50 installs a month in Japan not 5. Smaller companies always risk having to cover multiple tasks per person. The larger your business the more specialised your resources become; however, they may suffer more downtime as they wait for their specific tasks to be required. Start-ups often plan to be large and scale appropriately, which has its own challenges.

Finally, to be discussed at length in the chapter on products, average sales price can determine installation needs. If a salesperson sells two or three big solutions a year built around their plan or design, then they of course should be involved in, or in fact lead, the installation.

### Customer Support - Who you going to call?

The Ghostbusters were at least clear on their technical support expectation setting, they specifically wanted you to call them. What expectation have you set with your customer regarding support?

This is a critical decision and again it is down to focus and hours available.

Customer support comprises two key skill sets, product service and technical support. Product service people turn screwdrivers, or other tools to make equipment work or to ensure they function correctly (servicing). Technical support people attempt to understand problems during product use and help fix them. Questions can be answered by a mix of product knowledge and investigation. Normally this builds up the FAQ (frequently asked questions) section of a website, more commonly seen nowadays as stock answers when a chat bot is trying to direct you to a possible answer.

Product service repairs are relatively easy; if, after initial diagnosis, the product is confirmed as broken, it will need to be returned for further investigation. If possible, it will then be repaired, either under warranty or for a charge. The salesperson's job here should be connecting the customer to the service team.

If faults require onsite support, salespeople are rarely going to be able to help in any other capacity than getting the engineer a coffee. Of course, some can be trained to do board replacements, calibrations etc but really if it's a product service problem salespeople are out.

So, when are salespeople getting involved?

Product service is connected in most instances to manufacturing, they made the product so they will know what has broken from their plan. Technical support however is not connected to manufacturing although this is often where it ends up. In fact, the skill set required is more that of a product expert and product experts live in sales and marketing. Salespeople tend to end up getting involved because of a few key reasons.

### 1. Technical support is owned by the salespeople

In some organisations support is owned by the sales team - this is not necessarily start-ups or small companies, some large businesses have their regional salespeople do everything from finding the customer, selling, installing to support. In effect they are almost operating as if the salesperson is running a franchise business for a specific territory.

### 2. Salespeople know the answer

Some salespeople know their products and have the battle scars to prove it - many of them have survived their long service by helping customers and running long-term relationships. If they know the answer, they will help in preference to forwarding them on to another person to help, even if they cost 5 times less and need to learn and it's their job. You can't blame them, but in return they can't blame you if they miss quota because all these little bits of help added up to a large distraction.

### 3. Distrust in the technical support team

Sometimes the support team isn't good enough, people often try to merge product service and technical support and end up with screwdriver-based support people. These people don't have the experience to help customers trying to use products in a real-world environment - they only really understand how to check products using their test equipment to establish that they meet product specification tolerances. Support isn't about meeting specifications, service is.

Getting a sales team to trust a support team can take a long time. We should also remember when trying to improve such relationships that the external customer feedback is more important than the internal feedback. Unless you use customer-feedback data everyone is trading what they think, which is just poor science as neither party is consuming the service.

4. Distance from customer support

Time zones and language are obviously an issue for a global business, especially if you have not set up a global support network. I remember in my past having a support team on the East Coast of the USA - clearly for American customers this was fine, but for Europeans they were available 2 hours a day and in Asia they could only provide support by email and appeared to only work 3 days a week. As local salespeople we had no choice, we had to offer direct field support - if we could not answer from our collective local knowledge, we would use the East Coast support team to support us. It was not fun; you became a master of writing clear emails and every morning you checked your emails hoping that someone had picked it up and got you an answer. If not, the day was burnt, and you were back chasing in your afternoon and evening.

Some markets also need differing support because of language or culture. I had enough problems getting service teams in America to communicate correctly with Europeans; imagine how hard it would be for the Japanese.

Overall, salespeople end up taking on support because what is being offered by the business is simply not sufficient to allow them to function and they would fall well below market expectations without this. Some of this will need challenging but it needs to be approached with an open mindset. For example, if your European team wants to set up a local support team in Germany but will not sign up to increased sales because they now have X days more free time then that's unreasonable on their part. If you insist on your European customers contacting your US Support team first, in place of calling their local representative, then maybe it's you that is being unreasonable.

Most customers are going to need support in one way or another during the products use, even if it's just to ask a basic question. They genuinely do not care who gives them support if the person or method is competent and clear. They could be anywhere in the world, it could be the middle of the night, the customer just wants the information and to know how to restore them to a better place. I have multiple software subscriptions for tools I collect to make life easier, I've been in contact with many of them to ask questions and I'm sure not a single person online is in the UK. I don't care if they watched the game last night, I do care that they understand what I'm asking and can help me. Customers also don't mind waiting - what they hate is false hope.

So how are you going to set expectations and how can you help reduce the burden on your salespeople?

Some organisations make it clear; they have a menu item on the website called support - it can be simply a telephone number and contact form, or it can be diagnosis tools, frequently asked questions, videos explaining things.

Self-help material is great and comes from repetition of problems which you don't want to explain again. As an example, to make one of our products function you had to install Firewire PCI card. I got bored, and we shot a video of my colleague David plugging one in and explaining it. Now it must have been a problem for more than just our customers as over 65,000 people have watched us plugging a board into a PCI slot.

As with everything nowadays, the material is there but driving people to it is more of the issue. People want an answer fast. Self-service is a little slower and not immediate, however this can be addressed through expectation management with the customer. For example, I would not dream of asking Salesforce.com for support on my question - I would search the web and get results in the form of videos, tech notes and customer forums, I've learnt self-service from this company that we regularly cut 6 figure checks to. But try the same with SAP CRM, I can only assume the information to help me here is hidden in the bowels of the dark web because I found nothing useful online – only consultants have the answers to SAP.

Technical support staff are great at fixing broken items or advising on basic software functions or drivers. What they cannot be expected to know is applications, they are also not great at digging problems through to the end - here salespeople often end up with the problem. If it is a product being sold in volume, this should really be sent to engineering as part of a sustaining effort, but even to get to that point may need some explanatory work.

Years ago, I had a problem where a routine I had written in a software package crashed, there was no reason why it should crash. The software company could not replicate the error. We tried different computers, different number of loops, etc. I finally got the software company on a web meeting to discuss and show them my issue and - I'll be damned - it didn't fail. I said thanks, apologised and moved on. Next time I tried it failed - I wanted to check it again so got a colleague on a web meeting and again it worked. I spent the next day working out if it was me re-booting the machine or some other step. I could not get it to work so, one more web meeting with the colleague to discuss and it worked again. Turned out it was the web-meeting software - it was stealing a processor, for some reason the software was failing when using multicore machines and the software company could not replicate as they only used PCs with a single processor. A week burnt without sales.

So, you may end up with salespeople having to document odd errors or get involved some way. Applications and product specialists if you have them should own these tasks.

Job titles, as noted in chapter one, can mean many things to different people. On one trip to meet our new owners' Asia team managers, I was told that they have no need for support people, and they were amazed that we used them in our business. When I spoke to their applications people, they were all replicating support issues and fixing customer issues, same job - different name, sometimes even different department. This may have been different industry language; it may also have been to allow them to put the cost in a different bucket to meet their corporate required ratios or even the result of a lost battle of who owns the cost at a department head level.

Overall, I think technical support people are a different breed to salespeople, and someone in your organisation needs to be prepared to help customers, even at the end of a quarter when everyone is trying to close business. No matter how you choose to help customers just make sure you meet market expectations or define yours with the correct reasons.

Sales is always going to have some involvement with customer support - it is inevitable, but for the good of the customer and to give yourself a chance of growing, do minimise that involvement where possible. The nature of salespeople makes them second-rate support people – although of course you can give me exceptions. For me, get technical support as far away from your salespeople as you financially can afford to. In my experience, salespeople that owned support sat in limited growth businesses where the sales team serviced $1-2M a year and the number of reps never changed; it is a solution for a steady state business, not a growing one.

The danger of salespeople providing too much support is obvious - you reduce their ability to sell, specifically in the IDENTIFY and DEVELOP segments. This is not just through the increase in coverage required for the SERVICE segment where the support happens, but it's also the increase in requirement of the KNOWLEDGE segment. If you're going to let salespeople cover the SERVICE segment, then you're going to need them to have high levels of product, application, and domain knowledge. This costs you; either you need to pay for the experienced staff, or you need to pay while people are learning, possibly missing out on opportunities as they do.

*Customer Engagement – Just Checking In*

Hello, my name is Dave and I'm your new rep for…. Some customers love their rep. - this is normally a relationship thing. If they repeat-purchase, it's about trust. If it's a one-time buy, it's probably more about the experience. Some customers simply don't care. I liked the salesperson who sold me my last car - if he were in the showroom next time I'm looking for a car, I would walk straight to him. If he called me today, I'm uninterested as I'm not in the market for a new car at the moment.

Someone in your organisation needs to own the relationship with the customer, it could of course be a CRM based marketing machine pumping out update emails or the occasional farming call. But who is doing the follow up to see if I am happy? Who is seeing if I'm a promoter or a detractor? And is anyone planning on asking me for a reference or referral?

For the repeat customers purchasing parts, components, or consumables then this is normally covered. These customers are the life of the salespeople, they know the customer and communicate with them weekly or monthly. If you sell only a handful of big systems a year or simply work a few accounts, this is also easy for a salesperson to manage.

If you sell low price retail items, this will also be different. We purchased new school shoes for my son on Monday - one of (I'm sure) thousands of transactions that business did that day. They didn't seem to have a plan for follow up to measure my satisfaction, maybe they do this by monitoring complaints or take random samples. Of course, email marketing is open to them to get feedback but most of us now hate email.

But what about the large majority of technical salespeople who have average deal sizes in the region of $25-200,000? Here your salesperson will handle somewhere between 15 and 75 transactions a year depending on the products price mix.

In this situation, satisfaction measurement could be part of a customer service role based in operations or could be conducted by sales or marketing staff. It can also be, just like the shoe shop, where you can choose to not care or randomly sample satisfaction.

What we do know is that people who like your products a lot talk (promoters) and those that you've failed talk even more (detractors). There are various ways of measuring how to understand this -The standard one is the Net Promoter Score (NPS) developed by Fred Reichheld, he explains this in his book The Ultimate Question 2.0, another worthy read. If you have ever been asked to rank something out of 10, chances are this was for a NPS study.

So, we want to find satisfied customers not just to know how we are doing but also to help find the promoters and leverage them further. Selling is about risk reduction and comfort; people don't want to take chances and so any presentation from the customer is king. "Dear Prospect, I do what you do, have the same pains as you and this company/product made it better" – simple isn't it.

References, as I would annoy my salespeople by frequently saying, are written down to be shared, a reference not written down is simply a customer you like - if you can't leverage them liking you and your product, they add no real value. So, what needs writing down? Well, the story is one thing, which leads to the creation of content from which we can drive most value, but the other thing is the agreement - quite what is the customer agreeing to?

Does the customer agree to let the company use their name, company name, images, data? Does the customer agree to take calls to speak to prospects, agree to talk on a webinar or even show the products to interested parties? Once again just don't leave this floating, I guarantee you it will bite you in the bum.

So, we all know references are valuable but who collects them? Well, I've tried all sorts here with mixed results. Marketing communications I found were never technical enough, applications people were nice but often soft and salespeople, if good, were selling. However, all are capable, and someone needs to own reference collection and the sales or marketing leaders need to design and own the process. The reference from Boston can't look different to New York for example.

References are hard to get mainly because you're asking for a favour in most instances and customers like all of us, have stuff to do and you're just a distraction. The act of bothering and possibly risking relationships leads most salespeople to give up. Where possible I would make this a job of the applications person if what is needed is technical, or the job of an internal salesperson if it's simply procedural.

What about referrals, who owns them? Well, here I think this really needs to be at the salesperson level and can be an extension of farming or the local ground game.

What I would say is that of course some happen automatically but, in most instances, they probably need a nudge. Many years ago, I used to travel to Edinburgh (great city - do visit) to see a customer of one of my sales managers. The customer was in fact great fun, but one thing did niggle, why were we not winning Edinburgh, he knew everyone. One day at coffee I said to him "David, we come up here, we help your staff, we run courses, we provide good service, when are you going to start saying good things about us?" He was simply confused; he had never really thought about it. However, he got it and went on to become not only a reference but gave us a lot of referrals. Just remember - you are a small part of people's day and sometimes you do actually need to ask people to do things.

Obviously, there are other ways you can ask for referrals which can be done at a marketing or internal sales level, and normally these involve rewarding the referrer with a benefit. These are not really about recommending when you're 'wowed', more about recommended because the customer sees it as a win-win. For example, if you recommend our product to a colleague and they purchase we will give you X. X can be as simple as money, which many organisations may block or it can be an accessory, marketing swag or extensions to warranty or places on training course etc.

Many products do not wow; for example, you can get $100 for referring a friend to an internet provider. I'm not exactly wowed by my internet provider; I pay a lot of money and I'm happy if it makes a day without a drop. Of course, there is room with mass market products for manipulation - everyone needs the internet, so everyone just refers each other, we all get the $100 and we wonder why it's expensive.

*Warranty, Upgrades & Add-ons*

Warranty is effectively gambling. Just as with any insurance, I'm gambling that if I pay a small amount, I won't have to pay significantly more at the time it breaks, especially if I really need it working at that critical moment of failure. The small amount maybe for a piece of hardware, 10-20% of the new value of an instrument, or for a software product - this may be as much as 30% of the value. However, SaaS (software as a service) has persuaded most of us to subscribe our way to safety.

I could consider this as a positive, not difficult to offer, could add additional revenue, could be a nice top up. Alternatively, I could consider this as a waste of time and a distraction to my salesperson, who has a quota based on driving new product sales.

Again, there will be multiple factors that will affect this including market expectations, industry or business cultures relating to financial risk or the risk of that product failing to work - maybe your product is a vital cog in one of their processes causing multiple cascading delays and costs.

Twenty years ago, we sold warranty dressed up with some nice service and extras and managed to drive a nice 10% bump in revenue simply by effectively sending out letters and quotes to customers. Other companies I've worked for had more complicated offerings; we needed to contact multiple 3rd party vendors, estimate risk, build in service visits, calibrations, and acceptance tests. Clearly that was not just send a letter and collect the cash.

If you can deliver real value through warranty, then who is going to own this? If it's a letter, it could be your product service team, internal sales. If it is larger and needs more thought, is it better with a salesperson?

What about upgrades? Well, here you may be ensuring that a customer can keep using your product. For example, IT have just told them they are being moved to Windows 11; unless the customer purchases an upgrade to your product to make it function, their solution will fail to operate in future. All sounds reasonable - maybe this could be handled online or sold by an internal salesperson or team.

However, if your product is complex or integrated with other products then maybe upgrading one part may break another. For example, our product service team might sell software upgrades and we would then need to apologise when that stopped another connected 3rd party product working.

Controlling this risk is really going to be about how you share information, document, and train. I have horror stories where people would upgrade customer's software without telling me and then cost days to fix the changes. It doesn't mean that only experienced salespeople should sell upgrades – it means think about it and do things properly.

Now, upgrades in the situation above are related to upgrading what someone has in use – it does not mean replacement. When people say they've upgraded their car, they normally mean they got a new car and sold their old car – no new spoiler or low-profile tyres were added to their existing car. To be clear, here, if a product needs replacing, the only person to replace it should be the quota-carrying salesperson trained to do the job. We went through a nightmare period where our product service team sold customers replacement products, rather than passing the customers on to the sales team for re-qualification – it was a 'cluster★★★★'. The product service team in that instance were lacking in the required KNOWLEDGE segment.

Finally, what about add-ons? Just as with warranty, they typically are 10-20% of the value of the initial purchase, but critically extend or enhance the capability of their installed solution. Here, you need to assess how complicated the add-on solution being offered is. If it's in anyway complicated to explain, use, install or risks breaking the already installed solution, it should simply become part of the salesperson's product basket.

For some, the warranty, upgrades, and add-ons are nice little earners to help the salesperson get to target. As noted, several times now, change is hard for sales staff and taking anything away from them hurts. If we ask long service salespeople who should sell warranties, upgrades, etc, they are going to have their standard response (like a cave man banging their chest as they grunt out the words) – "Me – my customer."

Salespeople do not do this always through greed, with a view to a quick buck – a lot of it is due to a worry over control. They may view this as the first step in eroding their responsibilities or you messing up their market, reputation, and lifestyle.

All these concerns can be addressed with logic, teamwork, and financial motivation. For example, if we assessed that we wanted to grow 10%

through additional sales of small items to existing customers, then we should be able to fund it and we can link people and incentives together to make it work.

When I was in sales, I wanted the revenue and not necessarily the work that went with it. I think that if you can see a real win by selling such items, then commit to selling through internal sales or other dedicated sales channels.

My last point on all these post initial sale extras is that you're going to need a CRM to do the work for you, and not any old CRM but that rarest of things - a working one where sales use it correctly. CRMs only work for customer relationship management when they are made so easy to use that they are used accidently by salespeople - because it's easier to use the CRM than doing it any other way. You may also need to help sales by running hygiene reports and having dedicated CRM data hygienists. CRMs left uncared for are like teenagers' bedrooms.

Most CRMs fail because too many departments want to track or control things or want to create utopian processes to be smart and handle big data. What they forget is that big data is reasonable data viewed from a salespersons point of view and they are the people adding the data, it only becomes big data when all viewed together. If you are going to use a CRM, really commit time to simplification and removing items rather than adding them - remember a CRM is for salespeople, everyone else is just spying on their data to view trends.

| TACTICAL SUMMARY | |
|---|---|
| Installation & Training | Salespeople / Applications or Product Specialist / Support Team / DE-EMPATHISE |
| Customer Support | Salespeople / Technical Support / Product Service / Product Specialist / FAQ / Collateral / DE-EMPATHISE |
| Customer Engagement | Salespeople / Application Specialist / Product Specialist / Marketing Communications / Collateral / CRM / DE-EMPATHISE |
| Warranty, Upgrades and Add-ons | Salesperson/ Internal Sales / Dedicated Sales Team / Product Service / Customer Support / DE-EMPATHISE |

## CHAPTER SUMMARY

SERVICE can be considered as anything that happens with the customer post purchase. This can be completing contractual obligations (training, installation, and support), leveraging the new relationship (references, referrals) and selling additional products.

The key to successfully completing obligations is by setting and meeting expectations. This has the added benefit of helping create the vision of the solution in prospect's eyes during the DEVELOP segment.

Salespeople get involved in customer support for several reasons, some relating to the situation or the market but many due to mistrust in the existing support network.

Salespeople should, wherever possible, be removed from installation and support activities - however there will always be situations where sales are involved in support due to already established and nurtured relationships.

Someone needs to take ownership of customer relationships in your business post-purchase - this can be to ensure or measure satisfaction or to help provide meaningful feedback to the business.

In some cases, customer relationships can be converted to references and referrals, helping to grow sales further. To make these a success, a manager or leader needs to design the process, enforce standards, and ensure the program gets used.

Warranty sales are common in many markets and in many instances are an easy way to increase revenue and offer customers a higher level of service. However, salespeople may view this as an administration task which detracts from core product sales.

Existing customers are the most likely to buy additional upgrades and add-on products to increase functionality of performance. These sales are often of a lower average sales price and so may cause a distraction to quota carrying salespeople.

# Chapter 7: KNOWLEDGE

Knowledge is power, well that's if it is needed; if it's not needed or exploited it's a waste. Here we explore the segment in the SalesDISK© that serves the rest - KNOWLEDGE. What do you need to know to get the job done?

| SEGMENT | SUBSEGMENT | DEFINITION |
|---|---|---|
| KNOWLEDGE | Domain Knowledge | Knowledge of a specific discipline or field - for example, software as service, test equipment, pharmaceutical industry |
| | Territory Knowledge | Knowledge of the geographical region, the account locations, and customers within it |
| | Application Knowledge | Knowledge of job or task that the prospect is attempting to complete, having dealt directly with similar problem beforehand |
| | Product Knowledge | Knowledge of your products, their features and how customers achieve their results by using them |

Figure 7.1 - Subsegments & definitions of KNOWLEDGE

The key questions we need to answer are

- Is the knowledge important to you?
- If so, how do you plan to exploit it?
- Who in your business needs to have that knowledge?

The minute I meet someone new, my brain automatically searches for similarities; connection points that I can quickly feel comfortable with. This can be as an ice breaker or as a means of simply sustaining a conversation. I'm always jealous of those who follow football, something I loved playing but I never cared enough to be a fan of the professional sport. If you follow professional sport and know the names, scores, and history you can walk into a bar and start a conversation with anyone. My old president was a master of this, every time we travelled together I would arrange to meet Jim before dinner in the hotel bar where I would find him in conversation with some stranger discussing the ice hockey, football, baseball, basketball, anything really.

The same is true if you have ever belonged to a club, in some cases my club has been 'being British'. Travelling in America and Asia, any Brit I meet is an instant conversation - we identify and bond, if only for a moment. I'm in a military club because I love the military and was a reservist. I'm in a salespersons' club - I can meet salespeople and I talk the talk and share empathy and success and failure stories.

*Domain Knowledge*

Domain knowledge is the same to me, it's an ability to find instant rapport because we share frames of reference. If you've been around something whether it be an industry, a product, or an application for a number of years and know a bit about it, you've got domain knowledge. If you have domain knowledge you can not only get on with people, but you understand the rules of that domain.

For example, I have domain knowledge from years of selling to academic research accounts; I know how they work having been to research facilities in over 30 countries. I understand their layouts, how they are set up, how to find people, how people purchase, I even know how to get a parking spot. Is that important? In some cases, yes. If the job required me to understand how to sell to research institutes, I could take it on - I could sell anything from test tubes to mass spectrometers. How important it is to the sale? If I want to sell a product into the automotive industry, I would be less useful. I can learn and I can sell but maybe it's not worth it; better to find someone with the correct domain knowledge.

I also have domain knowledge of high sensitivity scientific grade cameras. I know the history, I know how they work, I know the pains of making them and what customers value. I may be useful in a sideways move to a camera sensor business, but I would need a lot of help in moving to selling laboratory reagents, cars, or finance software. Depending on the size of your market, the ability to find candidates with domain knowledge can vary. The more niche the market, the more you may need to borrow from adjacent markets, and even here it can be really hard work as you try to get them up to speed.

Some situations don't need that much domain knowledge. For example, when we sold products to OEM accounts, we added little value, they were their own market's domain experts not us. What they needed us for was our product knowledge.

Domain knowledge can be important in the IDENTIFY segment, helping the salesperson look in the right places, ask the correct questions to qualify the need and help build rapport and understanding of shared or overlapping experiences. Within the DEVELOP segment it can help with positioning and demonstrating capability.

We saw first-hand what domain knowledge could give you, we hired scientists to explain to scientists why they should buy our scientific products and it worked. Part of this was the domain knowledge but they also liked the applications and product knowledge. I have also hired people who sold less complicated commodity products with zero domain knowledge, it worked just fine.

If you decide you value domain knowledge but the incumbent salesperson is lacking or difficult what else could you use to fill the gap? Well applications and product specialist can help easily within the DEVELOP segment but it's a little harder to provide any meaningful value with tasks in the IDENTIFY segment. They or marketing can of course help create targets to call as part of prospecting or business development.

One last trick is to use imagery and language of the domain in marketing collateral to at least position your products within the chosen domain. For example, if I want to sell to the Automotive industry, I can use Shutterstock to obtain professional images of cars on production lines to help build the picture in people's minds.

*Territory Knowledge - It's not what you know, it's who you know*

Territory knowledge is knowledge of the people and places. Have you ever had a friend who was just connected? I've had a few - anything you want, they know a person. What about a friend who knew all the best places for dinner and drinks, all the city secrets? Territory knowledge exploits knowledge of both people and places.

I have a better understanding of the Tokyo metro system than I do of the London one. I know how to get about in Japan, how to act, how to get meetings and a little of the culture and history. I'm a big fan. I could be considered useful to people daunted by the idea of going to meetings in Japan.

In the same way my friend Matt knows the UK. He should do, he lives in it but he also knows all the worthwhile research accounts in the UK. And he knows people - if not the right people for your products, his relationships with those people could facilitate new desired ones. Matt has high territory knowledge. After 20 years in the region there is little he can't tell you about what is going on where.

I've made some bad hires based on presumed territory knowledge. We once hired a very nice person for Texas. They had strong domain knowledge, but we put too much faith in their territory knowledge, they knew the accounts, where to finding parking but not the people in the numbers we were going to need. In doing so we failed that person; they were not correct for the role.

I've worked in many situations where territory knowledge made the difference and added real value, but there were others where I would use salespeople to sell across the world with none; they didn't care if the prospect was in Boston or San Diego and other than time-zone differences, they made no effort to understand. Sometimes it matters, sometimes it doesn't.

Territory knowledge can be key to IDENTIFY segment. Many salespeople cover a region and the longer they stay in that region, the better their territory knowledge is, and the more they can exploit it for farming and prospecting. They make good use of the relationships, references, and referrals from the SERVICE segment. You can see this exploited a lot by long-service salespeople, they learn their patch and they make it work for them.

Imagine that you're starting a new business and you want to sell into an existing market but have no contacts, then a smart move is to hire someone with territory knowledge who can get you in the door.

If you're generating a large number of marketing leads, have chosen to service a wide region, or are running an internet or virtual sale, then territory knowledge will be less important to you.

What other resources could stand in for territory knowledge? Well, if you had a CRM with good customer data in, that could help a lot. When a salesperson leaves and you have a good CRM, you can give the replacement a head-start to get the territory going again. I knew a company once where a long-term, 30+ year sales legend retired, all the relationships were with him, all in his head. When he left, the data was in the CRM but not in any way that a report could ever be run in order to segment the contacts into customers, products, or applications. It was like having a rolodex of business cards where you had no idea why the salesperson had kept that business card in particular - nothing to say whether they were a customer or a prospect that they'd met for lunch once 20 years ago who'd purchased nothing.

Others in your company may have some territory knowledge which can be borrowed, or you may want to purposely hire locally positioned applications or product specialists who know or can learn the area through time spent demonstrating.

*Application Knowledge*

Similar to domain knowledge but not quite the same, application knowledge focuses entirely on the specific task to be completed by the customer using your product.

As an example, I have been involved in the installation and roll-out of a few CRMs in my time. I have little domain knowledge, I can list 3 or 4 CRM products, met a few people, watched a few videos, but not enough to hold a decent conversation for an hour on the matter. I know the basics of how they work, how to set them up but having been in sales and sales management for 2 decades I know a lot about how people would like to use them to do their jobs and so I have reasonable CRM application knowledge.

When I sold into scientific research, I would say that I had some application knowledge but I rather more got the general gist of the situation - I was more application apathetic. The applications people I hired though were at a different level, in that they could think on a different plane to me.

It took me about a year in sales to work out that I wanted to know only enough to make a sale. My interest was skin deep. If there was high investment required, I didn't want to know. For sure I wanted to know if an investment would lead to scale for selling, but really my core interest was purely sales-based success. It was not that I was not interested, more that I decided that knowing more on the matter would not necessarily lead to more sales.

I knew enough to understand pain points in a job, recognise them and sell to them. "Oh, you do job Y, well in that case don't you hate it when......" was very much my approach.

Some people just can't grasp even this level – I'm not sure if it's an intelligence thing or more a block in the same way that I simply don't understand electricity - people have tried to explain it, but my brain just stops.

For many businesses the salespeople have to own the application knowledge due to the nature, complexity or nicheness of their products. In these situations, people tend to hire for knowledge and train for sales. You can of course do the reverse, but you may end up with someone who is an idiot and can't understand how electricity works! Hiring for applications gives you a speed advantage - you're basically hiring a hunter-turned-gamekeeper; they can get to speed with product and demonstrations fast - there is time to sharpen the sales pencil later. Please be hyper-aware that you will give these people sales titles but often they will not fit the regular model of what you think a salesperson is and they will reside where you hired them, which is in a heavily weighted KNOWLEDGE segment. Don't be shocked when they don't prospect.

Just as with domain knowledge we can also use marketing to help within our sale, by providing application knowledge as a sales support tool. The concept can be as simple as having someone write associated articles, for example a technical note explaining the application and indicating which of your products to use. This can be backed up by reference to customers doing that job and even videos showing your product doing the job. The salesperson's required application knowledge can thus be reduced to a minimum, with the weight being carried by this added content.

*Product Knowledge*

How does it work? I always had a mild interest in *how* something worked but I had a real interest in *which buttons* made it work. They are different but they both form part of the product knowledge.

As an example, if I explain to you that in digital cameras there is a silicon sensor made of an array of pixels, that when photons hit the pixel they interact with the silicon creating electrons and that we can measure electrons and convert them to greyscales and we can then show those greyscales on a screen and voilà, we have an image.

Now firstly, physicists calm down – I was being simplistic! Secondly, I have no idea about the movement of the charge, how this is done, how the electrons travel down cables – I've got nothing. I know the basics; the engineers and product managers know the rest.

I knew enough of the background story – how it works, but I knew a whole load of the 'what buttons to press' side of product knowledge. I could demo. I could answer questions.

So how much about your products should your salespeople know – a little, enough to sell, occasionally bringing in an expert, enough to install?

If your product is complex and people need high product knowledge to sell it then just remember that they are trading the time against other segments on the SalesDISK©. You can't have a big KNOWLEDGE segment and then keep the others segments big also.

Where this knowledge gets used will be in DEVELOP and SERVICE segments. This is where demonstrating, answering technical questions and position over competitors can all be achieved by the salesperson. Deep product knowledge adds little or no value to the IDENTFY segment.

Applications specialists can be used here in place of salespeople. They know the product to a high standard – this is because they need to know how it operates on a daily level to complete demonstrations. Sometimes you may have dedicated product specialists; these people know fewer applications than applications specialists but they know enough. When the product is really technical they can be used, paired with a salesperson, to ensure that all the correct buttons are pressed and the harder questions get answered.

Product managers can also be used as product specialists; they know their products, but they have less available time because they must focus on their key tasks. If you need product support regularly then you need product specialists, if you need it occasionally then a product manager will make do. You may even need someone from engineering – but please take care of them, they are unused to daylight and get startled easily.

As I mentioned before, along with domain and application knowledge we can use marketing to reduce the burden of required knowledge from the salesperson. But the use of marketing collateral is, I believe, becoming a barrier rather than a leveraging benefit. Although it allows you to achieve the minimum customer expectation, only *outstanding* marketing collateral or tactics will stand above the rest. You can respond fast to articles, if a competitor writes an application note then five days later you can neutralise the impact with your own. Of course, you need your communication channels to be as strong or stronger than that of the competitor or it means nothing as no one sees it, leaving it as an objection-handling document.

The new challenge for all of us is controlling how the information and resources are deployed and accessed. We had references, articles, white papers, videos, etc on our websites that our sales either didn't know about or couldn't remember how to access. Making all this information useful to the salespeople as well as the prospects and customers is taking over as the challenge.

| TACTICAL SUMMARY | |
|---|---|
| Domain Knowledge | Salespeople / Applications or Product Specialist / DE-EMPATHISE |
| Territory Knowledge | Salespeople/ CRM / Other / DE-EMPATHISE |
| Application Knowledge | Salespeople / Application Specialist/ Marketing Collateral / DE- EMPATHISE |
| Product Knowledge | Salespeople / Application & Product Specialist/ Marketing Collateral / DE-EMPATHISE |

## CHAPTER SUMMARY

The KNOWLEDGE segment serves all the others within SalesDISK©.

Domain knowledge is knowledge of a specific discipline or field - for example, software as service, test equipment, pharmaceutical industry.

Domain knowledge helps build rapport and allows the salesperson to build credibility, authority and share frames of reference.

Domain knowledge best serves the DEVELOP and IDENTIFY segments.

Territory knowledge is knowledge of the geographical region, the account locations, and customers within it.

Adding staff with strong territory knowledge can help as a shortcut when entering a new market, allowing faster access by exploiting pre-existing relationships.

Territory knowledge best serves the IDENTIFY segment.

Application knowledge is knowledge of job or task the prospect is attempting to complete, having dealt directly with similar problems beforehand.

As with domain knowledge, application knowledge helps with authority and credibility, but it also helps position the product and build comfort for the customer.

Application knowledge best serves the DEVELOP and SERVICE segments.

Product knowledge is knowledge of your products, their features and how customers achieve their results with them.

High product knowledge helps within very complicated sales where there are deep questions about how the product works and how to use it

Product knowledge best serves the DEVELOP and SERVICE segments.

Marketing can be used to help present to prospective customers that the company possesses domain, application, product knowledge.

The SalesDISK© represents the focus and the resources but, be aware that if you require a high KNOWLEDGE segment, that will naturally reduce the size of all other segments. You can't have it all.

# Chapter 8: Deploying the SalesDISK©

In chapter one, I stated that SalesDISK© was designed to help your business in the following ways

- Review the main aspects of the sale so that the management team can prioritise the important and outsource or de-emphasise the rest
- Identify existing, and create desired Go-To-Market strategy
- Match the sales process to the customer buyer journey, while working within any company constraints
- Create efficiency and/or effectiveness of the sale to increase hit-rate.
- Create a companywide vision of the sale where everyone in the company understands their position
- Help specify staff to be hired and identify where training gives the most benefit

Really, we can see that there are 2 different areas in which SalesDISK© can help. The first 5 bullets refer to senior management strategy planning. The last bullet purely relates to the tool as an aid to hiring the correct people and getting them up-and-running fast.

Hiring people is changing. At the moment I'm witnessing a large turnover of people in sales positions, especially in my industry of scientific instruments and solutions. Why? Well people achieve things; you need people to get stuff done and so resources are in competition. The opportunity to jump and increase your salary by 10-20% has never been easier. Also, COVID-19 has forced a personal-time revolution – we all want to work from home and do more of our own things. We've seen the light of family and free time and want more.

Finally, I think people need more satisfaction. My generation was fixated on getting a job and paying bills. The later generations were more driven by adventure and interest. I even think that COVID-19 forced many in my generation (Gen-X) to consider what they were getting out of work aligning us with millennials and Gen Z.

So, what am I driving at? Overall if you hire someone into your business today, I expect them to stay between three and five years before they move on. With many this may even just be two or three years. I think this needs to be planned for in your recruiting strategy. Now of course some people stay for years, my previous company was littered with people who were 10–20-year veterans, I was one. I know you also can give me more examples, but please be assured that this is changing. People stay if you can keep them moving, upping their challenge, upping their responsibility. This is nice but it is impossible to do it for everyone. I've read recently about 'tours of duties' within companies, here people are moved through departments giving them experience and empathy, prepping them for business leadership – sounds great, sounds exclusive.

My expectation is that hiring is going to increase because staff turnover is going to increase. What's needed now is to make the process of hiring to outcomes incredibly efficient. Put it basically, you need to know what you want, get what you want and push the focus from day one. Now, of course the old adages still hold "hire for attitude" "hiring is guessing, firing is knowing" – all true, nothing changed but you just know that the value of an employee is needed faster than ever before. Needing value from an employee faster means knowing clearly what you want before you start. In my time, I've spoken to a lot of directors about hiring sales staff and I can sum up their needs into the following categories

1. Another of the same (preferably more like Dave than John)
2. Someone to do sales (I don't understand it, aren't they all the same)
3. Someone to get in there and make some calls (I desire activity, activity makes me happy)
4. Someone to work it out for me (I have no idea; I'm paying them to work it out)
5. An all-star (I believe people exist who can do it all and want to work for us)

Now this is a generalisation. I'm not trying to be rude but only when really quizzed out do you get better answers. This is because people are not very good at articulating their needs and sales is often considered an art. It can be an art but just remember it's actually a science. Only those good at the science can make it look like an art (even when they don't know they are).

Recruiters live the problems of poor definition relating to sales staff daily and I too have been guilty. The best recruiters have the experience to question you out about your needs. Why? Because they need to show you as close as possible to what you want, in order to get paid.

In established businesses, sticking to the past and rehiring the same is the most common route because it's low risk, you're unlikely to get fired by sticking to someone else's plan. This can either be because it works or because the leaders are not leading but managing. Remember leaders invoke change - that's their job. Managers do what I call weather-forecasting, they simply tell you what is happening short-term. Not how they are altering the world to make the correct things happen.

Now don't get me wrong, the world needs managers. I just have problems with people who think they are leaders and want the pay cheques of leaders, when they are in fact mediocre managers and oh my, are there a lot of jargonating pretenders out there.

So, what's the difference? Well, this is my take. You normally have to be both a leader and a Manager and what you have is actually different leadership or management tasks as shown in figure 8.1.

| LEADERSHIP TASKS | MANAGEMENT TASKS |
|---|---|
| **Establish Direction** <br><br> • Creates Vision <br> • Clarifies the big picture <br> • Sets strategies | **Planning And Budgeting** <br><br> • Establishes agendas <br> • Sets timetable <br> • Allocates Resource |
| **Aligns People** <br><br> • Communicates goals <br> • Seeks commitment <br> • Builds teams, coalitions, and alliances | **Organisation And Staffing** <br><br> • Provides structure <br> • Hires new positions <br> • Establishes rules and procedures |
| **Motivates And Inspires** <br><br> • Energises <br> • Empowers subordinates and colleagues <br> • Satisfies unmet needs | **Controlling And Problem Solving** <br><br> • Develops incentives <br> • Generates creative solutions <br> • Takes corrective actions |

Figure 8.1 - Leadership & management tasks

Some people exist only as managers. Only when they pretend they are leaders do they become the weather-forecasters I speak of. Typically, these people attend lots of meetings, are always busy, sometimes talk a good game, but can never give you an example of making change or of stepping over the line to deliver change.

Regardless, you need to be a top manager and a top leader. To keep on track, check what you're doing against my Leadership and Management Checklist in figure 8.2.

| LEADERSHIP CHECK LIST | MANAGEMENT CHECKLIST |
|---|---|
| Are you communicating your plan and the overall company direction? | Are you communicating consistently? |
| Do people know their place within the plan? | Are you spending the correct amount of time on what is needed? |
| Are you coaching? | Are you assigning tasks to ensure that you have time to do the most vital, hardest, world-changing tasks? |
| Are you thinking in the background about your staff's next steps, skills, and talents? | Are your team doing what you need in order to achieve your goal or their sub goal? |
| Do you discuss your plans with your team? | Are the tasks and timescales for tasks clear? |
| Are you thinking about change and driving real change? | Are you holding people to account? |

Figure 8.2 - Leadership and management check list

As noted, as a leader you are going to have to drive change. So, what do you do when you finally have to change sales strategy? Well firstly, take advice. Don't be proud. Read books. Watch YouTube videos. Discuss with people in other markets. Talk to independent consultants. What I really want you to avoid is hiring people without a plan or with only half a plan. It's not fair on them and it rarely works - you're just going to spin your wheels.

Using SalesDISK© as a template, starting with the segment view and moving to deeper questions we can really start to explore and develop your sales staff's needs. SalesDISK© helps you articulate what you actually need by limiting the choice and terms for discussion.

So SalesDISK© helps generate the needs for the hire, and sharpens the focus, so that when a person comes on board you can get them running faster.

Not only that, SalesDISK© has given you focus, and you can now identify where you can a add value by training them. This is important. When people start, they normally get a PC, branded water bottle etc and, if they're lucky, a plan. There are 50 things to train the person on and the entry period is a bit of a honeymoon. Within 6 months you could probably expect them to be running at 50% of value and at a year closer to 90%. Now that you only have two to three years with people, you can't wait for them to get running. You need a process to get people in and running and get them to 90% in less than 90 days.

By really tightening the focus on the jobs to be done SalesDISK© accelerates the training that they actually need. For example, if you have already decided applications people own the product and application knowledge, the product training for sales is not 'how to use', it's 'how to sell and where to look'.

To boost sales, you can now pick the relevant sales training method to use. That's right - pick a sales training model. I say this because salespeople tend to discuss sales training models as the religion they practice. Truth be told they all do different things. If you're focusing on the DEVELOPMENT segment you need one set, IDENTIFY another, etc.

*Sales Methodologies*

DEVELOP Segment

Sales methodologies – Solution Selling, Needs Selling, Conceptual Selling (PAIN), Value Selling
Aim – Developing needs or identifying pain points to develop or position your solutions. The goal is to understand the prospect and then provide solutions that solve problem/pain. Develop pain enough and the prospect will do anything to remove it. Relationship development is key, so that the prospect believes that you care about their problem.

IDENTIFY Segment

Sales methodologies – Challenger Sale, Adaptive Selling
Aim - Prospects do not realise the issues that they face. You are aware of them and develop pains/needs based on insights to problems.

SERVICE Segment

Sales methodologies – Solution Selling, Needs Selling, Conceptual Selling (PAIN) Value Selling, Challenger Sale
Aim - The salesperson is developing a relationship with your existing customer keeping your company relevant past the initial sale. The customer views your salesperson as an external consultant member of their business. Tactics include asking for referrals, watching customers use their equipment to perform their jobs, helping identify new sales opportunities, keeping customer informed of promotions, new products, etc.

KNOWLEDGE Segment

Sales methodologies – FAB Selling, Value Selling, USP Selling
Aim – Product-based sales focus on product-centric sales meaning there is great emphasis on features, advantages, benefits (FAB). Sale process is focusing on benefits.

STRONGMAN© is the only sales training model we see that fits across all segments. For me it's the one that is consistent across all businesses and really drives hit rate increases and forecast accuracy. This is because it focuses on the sale in play and what is needed to move it forward,
So, SalesDISK© can help to communicate your plan for hiring staff and help you to focus your training to get value from your new salesperson faster.
But.... were you correct in what you were asking for?
SalesDISK© helped by forcing thought of what is needed when specifying and hiring the ideal candidate, but was this thought based on the correct ideas? Does everyone agree with the sales director? Do we have alignment? Will this be correct in 3 years? Is it designed to fix problems or develop opportunities?

This is why SalesDISK© is bigger than just job specifications. It's about really getting in and getting you to consider the actual mechanism and plan for the sale. It's about thinking about who your company is, what you want it to be, and how you're going to drive it to that place.

This is not a few hours; this is an investment in SalesDISK© as a tool to keep you focused and on task to push you to really consider options and deliver outcomes. Here someone needs to own it. It can be the VP, director, manager or owner. It can even be an external consultant. If you want change then you need to make it happen.

*Next Steps*

The next few chapters are designed to help you consider the larger picture and again, to create the thoughts for you to delve deeper. If you want to be a weather forecaster then please put the book down and go back to your life of happy plodding. If you're inquisitive, read on.

## CHAPTER SUMMARY

The SalesDISK© is designed to help a business in many ways, however this can be simplified into 2 key areas. 1. Hiring better people to have impact. 2. Setting up your business to have better impact.

The job market is changing, post COVID-19 people are changing the way they see their lives and as companies fight for growth the competition for resources grows stronger. As a result, staff are going to turn over faster.

This faster staff turnover needs to be built in. Companies need to take this on board and use SalesDISK© to drive focus in the job to be done in order to maximise the speed from hire to value. There will no longer be honeymoon periods.

In established businesses we can often see repetition in hiring as people look to avoid change and to just go with the flow. Remember leaders are brought in to drive change.

Avoid being a weather forecaster who reports what is happening but rather do what is needed to change that for the better.

With a SalesDISK© in place, you can now provide the relevant training. As focus has been placed on a particular segment, we can now pick the relevant sales training model to use.

SalesDISK© helps create focus when hiring new sales staff but what about changing the bigger picture, What about the Go-To-Market strategy in general? Please read on.

# Chapter 9: Markets

- How do I define my market?
- How big is my market?
- Which markets do I want to serve versus skim?
- Can I copy/paste my model between markets?
- What aspects of the market will impact my SalesDISK©?

*Defining a Market*

Normally markets are defined by a mix of industry, region, or target organisation size, for example, selling widgets to small-to-medium enterprises in Norway. But how do we know Norway is a separate market to Sweden for example?

A market or marketplace can be defined as a place where people gather to buy goods and services. This has clearly expanded a little since what, in my head, conjures up the thought of a medieval village market.

Let's assume there is a physical market (fresh vegetables, meat, etc) in town A and another one in town B, just down the road. Suppliers go to both markets. One theory and one that I like (credit to my friend Rob) is that if customers go to both markets and discuss prices, quality, and availability, the markets are conjoined.

Marketplaces are separate if people do not communicate between them. If I sell a product in America, you can self-define this as the Americas market, however if the customers in America are in good communication with those in Europe and discuss things then really the market is now a conjoined American and European Marketplace.

In reality, customers who purchase cars in the US are probably not heavily in communication with those in the UK, so they can be considered separate markets. Those who work in medical research on the other hand are highly globally linked as they collaborate on finding solutions. Here your Go-To-Market and also your SalesDISK© could very simply be copy/pasted from the US to Europe.

With the internet you can argue that everything is now more global. This is probably truer now than ever, especially in comparison to 20+ years ago when I started.

There do remain some nice boundaries to keep things apart such as culture, language, currency, tax etc. As an example, you could say there is a global market for cancer drugs because people discuss their ordeals in globally accessible Facebook groups. However, the Food and Drug Administration has self-protecting rules which can force America to be a separate market.

*Regional Variation vs Territories*

Some markets are global, for example Starbucks or McDonalds. Now I've been about, and I've been to McDonalds in Japan, America, Canada, China, Peru, Spain, Portugal, Singapore, India, Costa Rica, UK. I know - classy, right? The branding is the same but there are local delicacies. Now I can imagine that you're thinking 'oh yeah, McDonalds China has all manner of different things'. No, I was actually thinking of the lobster roll they have in New England. Branding can be global but often regional differences exist.

You also get points for serving global markets in local ways, even being from the area helps. I spent a large chunk of my working career in America. I was allowed, people were nice, some people clearly did not understand why I was there as opposed to an American. We spoke the same language despite the whole aluminium thing, but my connection was token.

I would never be fully accepted - why? Because I never saw some guy kick a goal or drop a catch in some sport I have no concept of. In the same way that they will never remember Paul Gascoigne crying and Gary Lineker turning to Sir Bobby Robson and saying, "have a word with him".

People like local. If you cannot be local, be token. I got more meetings from being from out-of-town and only appearing for a few key dates than by being constantly available. Anyone booking meetings with a manager or applications expert should be masters of this.

Local markets also form for service reasons. A very smart consultant called Stephen used an example to explain this. He pointed out the difference between wanting someone to clean his house and wanting something to clean his house.

The "something" can be purchased online - a vacuum cleaner for example can be purchased anywhere. Normally it's within a country but I don't care - I'm sure the vacuum cleaner company has local distribution or a local office but that's not the point, that's an organisational choice. The "someone" to clean the house has different criteria and forces me to use 'local'. Services and the people who perform them can add value and create localised markets.

So, is your market local or wider? Let's consider Europe. Are France and Germany separate markets for your products? Well, a good way to tell is that if people in France only source those products in France, then that normally indicates that it's a local separate market.

Importantly sales territories are not markets. Sales territories serve local customers through local service. Putting someone to run the northeast of the USA is a tactical decision which supports and serves access to a local market or a set of customers in the main defined market.

I, and you, can, and of course do, exist in multiple markets. I may be part of a local market for one aspect and a global one for another. For example, when creating references discussed in the SERVICE chapter, we found that references served two markets - the broader regional one and the narrower global markets. For example, I am a Bostonian and I endorse Company J. If you are in Boston, they can help you. I am a Global thought leader, based in Boston, with problem Y that many of us have discussed and I have been helped by Company J.

A salesperson managing a territory in Boston will be serving the local marketplace and segments of other markets. These of course can be considered multiple segments of your key selected market.

*Same Job - Different Reason*

If some people buy my product for job A and others for job B and they talk to each other, then they are the same market; if they don't, they can be considered separate markets. In this way a market can be divided by customer application.

If people buy the same product for the same job but for different reasons even though they are in the same market, e.g. if one person loves the way a car looks and the other the way it drives, if they talk then it is one marketplace.

This is important as it forces some markets to coalesce. I once declared a market for my products to be used to do application A, but they worked in a building with people using it for application B, they were different - one preferring the quality and the other the speed, but they talked and were at similar events etc. They had different applications but as they communicated, they could really have been considered as one market.

## How Big is your Market? – Market Size

Calculating market size is very important and often confused.

Let's suppose you are in the UK, and you're selling a product successfully locally. You can of course sell it globally if it makes sense, but if you're simply selling when a person calls from the US you are skimming the US market, not serving it.

The coffee industry is worth $160 billion. If I sell coffee from my house who am I serving? Well people who walk past my house. Maybe my coffee is good, and people talk about it. What I'm not doing is saying I'm in a $160 billion Market. Starbucks however, are. Why? Because they have created a brand and process to serve customers around the world with consistency, and these customers interact. A local Starbucks store is however only serving local people or passing traffic.

My theoretical coffee shop is a good example. As I'm not really in the coffee market, I'm more likely to be in the 'refreshing people on the way to work' market. This is important because people assume that only their direct competitors comprise a market. As an example, we are company A, and we have competitors B and C. We overlap products by about 80% so market size is A + 0.8\*B + 0.8\*C. This sort of makes sense. However, customers to my coffee shop could have also purchased a bottle of water from the shop down the road. This is critical, markets are made up of competitors who solve the same problems you are solving – only not necessarily by solving it in the same way as you.

## Channel and Market Confusion

You can, of course define markets as you like, but be careful not to define a market as a channel. One pet hate of Rob and mine was people calling OEM a market. OEM is a channel. It can, and should, have a separate plan but based on product not marketplace.

You can segment them to be helpful. If a company makes a box for job Y using technology Z, then it's their market rather than yours. What we have is a product segmentation in our market being used to serve their market. We can't really affect their market, but we can build better products to help them – with higher capability, or lower price etc.

I like Rob's definition of market as: it has nothing to do with us the vendor, it is created through shared need and consideration. Knowing where and how your customers interact, and in what segments, is vital for Go-To-Market. As noted in virtually every book you will read about business, and in the film 'Star Wars: A New Hope', if you want to have impact you have to "stay on target."

In the early days of a market however, this can be hard to define as it may have applications in multiple markets not all communicating with each other.

*Early and Late Markets*

Humans and normal camera detectors can see colours between 400 and 700nm; anything below this is the UV (good for inspecting tiny faults in things like processors) and anything above is far red and then infra-red. IR Imaging is well known as we see it on TV footage from police helicopters or military raids. We think more of it as thermal imaging. Although thermal imaging or IR imaging for inspecting is common and a growing market. A company I worked with focused on ultrasensitive camera devices and developed an ultra-sensitive version of these products. The product was launched on the strength of the existing market served by simpler tech and lower cost products.

After a good launch, performance flattened out so we reviewed the leads and opportunities in the CRM and found that the applications were varied and the customers were all experimental users developing techniques and not following others. The markets were small, diverse and not quite ready for the revenues we believed we could extract. Being around in early markets can be really good to help establish positions, but they will often require a direct sales force to carry the message in order to grow. More time needs to be spent in the IDENTIFY and KNOWLEDGE section to find an understand these prospects if you want to grow.

As markets mature, and so long as the market is large enough, chances are you will need to shift to add focus to the DEVELOP and SERVICE segments.

*To Serve or Not to Serve*

Go-To-Market is about setting focus. You set the markets you can serve so that you do the least amount of work and take the least amount of risk. You can of course choose to skim some markets rather than dedicate resources to them.

Market skimming is the reverse of committing focus – it's being uncommitted to a market; it's not your core market but you will service requests as they come in with minimum effort.

To skim a market or not is an important decision. If you're skimming, your salespeople will do their best to handle requests as they come in, but I've seen it become a rabbit warren for many to get lost in. Normally this is because the product is probably being bent into the new application or the salesperson becomes over interested.

The final nail in the coffin for skimming is that your salespeople don't talk the talk – especially against competitors who are not skimming, but who have done the hard work, studying the market and learning the needs. Selling outside your initial or core market provides an excellent way to grow. Just be careful that it's conscious and not the result of skimming.

Skimming other people's markets is exactly how it should be presented to sales. If you don't ensure that your salespeople realise that these are just passing opportunities, they will be considered a massive upside to fix their numbers, providing false hope. Marketing's job is to have identified these markets and to have researched them, creating all the information to validate if entry is viable and profitable. What is to be avoided is salespeople going off on side missions which risk them hitting their forecast, quota, or goal.

Skimming means distraction for sales, but for marketing it represents an opportunity to investigate outside the core for new possible growth opportunities. This is business development as discussed in the DEVELOP segment chapter.

It is equally important to inform salespeople of the intention to move markets, so they don't see it as another skim.

Finally, do not confuse special projects with skimming. If something mega comes up, it needs to be worked as a group and should really be taken out of the existing quota agreement. The salesperson now fulfils a different role in the sale, normally local communication, and product managers, directors etc should come in to take ownership.

*Dark Territories*

We are always going to end up with dark territories, classic examples are Lithuania and Japan. For many, Lithuania would be too small to be considered independently or as an area of focus.

Japan on the other hand is large and a desirable land of opportunity for many. However, Japan had Sakoku (closed country) meaning that it was effectively shut to other countries from 1639 to 1853. This really changed the culture at multiple levels relative to the West, more so than any other country I've visited in Asia. Sales tactics and distribution truly need to be different because the buyer journey is so different; there are high levels of channel complexity with many layers, much of which is down to a high requirement for service. You may find it extremely hard to copy/paste your sales strategy here.

Japan's differences to the West also means it may not be part of many other conjoined markets you define. It is common for example, for scientists from Germany, UK and USA to collaborate or even share communication methods like Twitter, making them a market. Japan has far less overlap and does not use Twitter in the same way, so it's a distinctly separate market.

Cultural differences exist everywhere but to be honest dressing up markets in Europe or America as different based on cultural, or in the case of Europe language differences, is a thing of 20 years ago. By this I mean sales models can be copy/pasted across with minor nods to local language or interface differences. (can everyone please just use the same plugs!)

For dark territories special measures are needed. For many Lithuania would be handled by a salesperson in the UK, Scandinavia, or Germany, simply servicing incoming demand as it arises. Alternatively, a local dealer can help by servicing and creating additional opportunities and providing an easier purchasing route.

For Japan serious thought is needed. If you want to make a real difference and have scale, you should commit, knowing that you may be locally unprofitable to start. Alternatively get a distributor. To assist the sales team, marketing & support will need to adjust messaging, packaging, service times, materials, etc. All may need to be different in order to address the truly different market needs. Whatever you do with Japan, don't put your toe in the water and then change your direction every 5 minutes. Roots take a long time to take hold in Japan.

*Knowledge to Serve Multiple Markets*

Your business can of course serve multiple markets within one geographic area but can your salespeople cope with the different dynamics? Is there a benefit to having high domain knowledge?

I've witnessed this first-hand and it's a tough call to make. If the KNOWLEDGE segment is important, which one domain or product? For example, assume that you have a wide basket of products, 20 salespeople and you're serving 2 markets. Is it better to have 20 salespeople who are high in product knowledge and ok with domain knowledge - or 2 teams with high domain knowledge and reasonable product knowledge specialising on a market each?

For one business I had two teams, one covering Physics customers and the other Biology. Their product ranges overlapped by about 70% so there was no real product knowledge barrier. It was considered that domain and application knowledge were more important that product knowledge.

Domain knowledge is probably preferable if IDENTIFY is the key segment of focus, whereas product and application knowledge are better for the DEVELOP and possibly SERVICE segments.

*SalesDISK<sup>©</sup> questions*

1. Does your existing model work for your current markets?
2. Are your markets early (IDENTIFY) or mature (SERVICE and DEVELOP)?
3. Does your market need feet on the street (SERVICE and IDENTIFY)?
4. What subsegments are affected by your market? Example, how you demonstrate capability
5. Can you copy/paste your SalesDISK<sup>©</sup>s for California to Denmark?
6. Do you need multiple SalesDISK<sup>©</sup>s to serve multiple-markets due to KNOWLEDGE segment differences?

## CHAPTER SUMMARY

Markets are usually defined as a mix of industry, region, or target company size.

Markets can be considered the same if customers who exist in both markets talk to each other and share information.

The internet has broken down some barriers to markets, but there are still some barriers in place to keep markets separate. Some of these are functional and some are intentional.

Sales territories are not markets. They are set up to most efficiently or effectively serve customer needs based on geography.

Market definition is essential to help size your market. Within a market you will have direct competitors who look like you and others who solve the same problem as you plan to but with different solutions.

Markets which are late or early have very different needs. Early markets often need to be serviced directly whereas later markets are often serviced by greater efficiency or dealer channels.

Salespeople need to know which markets are core (in the plan) and which are skims.

Different markets may need different tactics, for example you may not be able to copy/paste your SalesDISK© for Europe to Asia.

In some cases, the market domain knowledge required may require you to segment your sales teams for the best results.

# Chapter 10: Products and Values

- How complex is your product?
- How niche is your product?
- Is it a solution, component, or commodity?
- What is your sale value proposition?

*Complexity-of-use*

The complexity-of-use is a bit of a funny term, but I am using it because complexity-in-product does not really have major impact. As an example, a laptop is an incredibly complex piece of technology. Yes, I'm sure you can tell me about RAM, operating systems, motherboards, buses, and I'm sure you could assemble one from parts available online. However, it remains easy to use.

When I got this laptop, the one I'm writing this book on, I did not have to understand how to turn it on, how to install programs, how to find the browser, how to connect to the internet. My history and its GUI made the job easy. A laptop is complex, the use of a laptop is not. If your product is easy to use then you may be able to utilise simpler selling models such as web-based-selling, but this is by no means guaranteed.

We would regularly fall down this hole. Our customers used our highly sensitive cameras to image cells changing during an experiment. If the software to control the camera and associated equipment was easy, this made the demo and eventually the sale easier, but it did not change the need of the customer to see the solution working with their specific cells in their environment (lab).

This is the same as a Ferrari, I imagine there is a wheel and associated pedals like my existing car, however, before I buy one and spend a house worth of cash, I would want to drive it.

Complexity-of-use can drive different segments of the SalesDISK© depending on your situation, maybe it needs a product and person present for a demonstration driving the DEVELOP segment, maybe there is a strong need for installation, set-up, and training, driving the SERVICE segment. Maybe it requires high product or application knowledge driving the KNOWLEDGE segment. Rarely do I see complexity-of-use impact finding projects (IDENTIFY).

149

## Task Environment Complexity

You may have a relatively easy-to-use product, but does it sit as a small thing in a complicated process? You may design the simplest-to-use device but if there are upstream or downstream complexities, this can cause more complications.

As an example, we would design the easiest-to-use camera devices – very few modes, exposure times and some trigger cables. Their use was uncomplicated but the use of them in the grand scheme of what was needed as a solution, was really complicated.

Customers wanted integration, which caused complications. Their samples and experiments were complicated - in some cases the experiments would cost thousands in reagents and take hours to run.

You may have designed a very simple-to-use product, but if the environment and jobs it is used for are not simple you may need to re-think how it's sold.

I'm sure the software that run space craft appear easy to use for the astronauts, just because it's easy doesn't always mean it's a phone sale or web video.

## Solution or Commodity?

How a product is sold will depend heavily on how it is viewed by the purchaser. There are some sales which are clearly a solution sale, for example adding a new nuclear powerplant is not a commodity sale, I hope it would involve many people and lots of meetings.

In the book "Solution Selling, the Strongman Process" by Ed Wal he separates solution from commodity by assessing the buyer's perception shown in Figure 10.1.

| | COMMODITY | SOLUTION |
|---|---|---|
| BUYING INTENT | IMMEDIATE FIX | LONG TERM SOLUTION |
| COST PERCEPTION | PRICE DRIVEN | VALUE AND INVESTMENT |
| VISION | HISTORIC | FUTURE |
| RELATIONSHIP | VENDOR ON DEMAND | BUSINESS PARTNER |
| BUYER SITUATION | SURVIVAL | LEADERSHIP |
| IMPACT | INSTANT | INSPIRATION AND STRATEGIC |

Figure 10.1 - Buyer's perception of a commodity versus a solution ("Solution Selling, the Strongman Process" by Ed Wal.)

Solution selling, as with my example of selling a nuclear powerplant, is going to take longer than any commodity, in theory. As an example, I do not over think my chocolate bar purchase. If I'm hungry I pick quick.

One problem that I faced in the past was that depending on the direction of the wind, customers would perceive some of our products as a solution or a commodity. As if this wasn't enough off a problem, our weakest salespeople did also. Some salespeople just quoted >$100,000 pieces of equipment with zero understanding of need, etc. If you don't capture the need you don't know how to position the solution, so it must be a commodity.

To force the products to be seen as a solution we deliberately made some sections of selling harder, to try to force better discussion of value, to build the solution argument. For example, in the early 2010s we had a product range which was as good as and possibly better than our competitors, but we were really just considered a third quote to be used to meet required purchasing rules. We would refuse to issue quotes without discussion and normally would reject their selected solution until we had discussed the need in depth.

Customers would call us and say "I need a quote for product A", we would ask "what's the application?" and they would say "it's application Y". "For Y you need product B, why would you want A, tell me about it". We would probably end back at product A but at least we understood the needs and had a chance to establish value.

We knew that if we were to win, we needed a fair battle ground - which was the demonstration. If we got the demo, we were >75% likely to win. This was costly and uneven as the other competitors rarely demonstrated, but we needed to overcome a speedbump and build a position so that we too could live off installed reputation.

Let's compare this to buying an airline ticket. I want to go from London to New York. I can fly British Airways, United Airlines, American Airlines, Virgin Atlantic, Delta and many more but it's a commodity – I go to their websites, specify the time and date and it gives me options. The market is so commoditised that Expedia exists showing me multiple prices and letting me pick on the lowest denominator - price.

At no point did the United Airlines website recommend I try the seats. As a side note, I fly United flying West and Lufthansa East. Why? Loyalty, they found a better way to attract me and manipulate this near perfect example of a price driven market.

Commodities are more likely to automate sales using web interfaces. Salespeople are more likely to be sales assistants helping with transactions. In the modern world I see this as the job of live chat - a tool I regularly enjoy if it is operated by a real person and not a chatbot. Businesses can also choose to sell products as if they are commodities to one group and as solutions to another. As an example, if I want to purchase one Salesforce.com licence I will be treated as a commodity; but if I want 1000, I get different treatment as now it's a solution.

If you have a commodity, service the sale. Use salespeople as assistants to reduce the friction of the transaction.

The more you believe your products are a solution, the more likely you are to favour a mix with higher DEVELOP and KNOWLEDGE segments.

*Components*

Components can be either a solution or commodity. You may sell a small widget which is $50 and available from a hundred vendors or a vital piece of tech which makes up 30% of the instrument's final cost, which you or only a handful of companies make.

There are also situations where a product can exist completely independently as a solution for one customer and as a component for another. We had products which we sold direct to end-users, but the same products were integrated into polished solution systems by VARs and also used by OEMs embedded within systems.

Our brand was useful for end-user and VAR sales but added little value to the final consumers of the OEM solution as they were totally unaware that we were ever involved. The OEM did however care about our brand, but the value proposition was different to that of an end-user as was the SalesDISK$^{©}$. They cared about the brand as it helped build a picture, and feeling, of quality, service, reliability, position, and history. All the things you're going to need because you can't risk delays or failures from your key suppliers.

How this drives the focus of your SalesDISK$^{©}$ again is dependent on your situation. Maybe for your $50 widget the demonstration of capability may be simple and so devalue the DEVELOP segment, maybe the failure of the part is critical and so you need to focus on SERVICE segment. The KNOWELDGE segment is also sometimes key as the customer wants a really intimate relationship with people of high product knowledge.

*Nicheness*

Identifying customers requiring socks should be easy. Having a product with mass market appeal often drives a clear model, online or in-store. For socks, I can purchase them from Amazon, or I can go to a department store, or as a final option wait for Santa at Christmas. Cars on the other hand are traditionally sold in showrooms with the very normal test-drive demonstration. There is little need for sales to focus on the IDENTIFY segment in the sock or car industry at an end-user level; there is probably more focus required on the DEVELOP and SERVICE segments. This is shown through the test-drive, the complicated configuration tools where I can pick the paint, trim, wheels, etc. The SERVICE segment is well managed with a person calling me every 6 months telling me about a new model, backed up by marketing, reminding me to come in for its annual check-up. They nurture me like crazy. Based on this there is a 50% chance my next car will be from the same company as my last.

Socks have less KNOWLEDGE segment requirement than cars, but they may slowly merge as the car industry is reducing its need for the KNOWLEDGE segment from the golden age of motoring simply because it is no longer required.

Niche solutions are sometimes niche because the market you're selling into is new and sometimes because the market is established but just small. In each case you're probably going to be selling direct and you're probably going to need to drive the IDENTIFY and KNOWLEDGE segments.

IDENTIFY segment. Important when it's a high-value solution as you're going to need salespeople to find prospects because the chances of marketing getting enough attention is always hard.

KNOWLEDGE segment. Important when the solution needs to be explained by people who understand the needs of the customer, having faced the same or similar issues themselves. Hunter turned gamekeeper is a classic approach. Who can explain it? Well, the guy from the last place we installed one.

*Variation*

Selling one product makes you an evangelist; selling two makes you a consultant. This is a very important statement, not only can having multiple products introduce multiple price points but you may need to sell them in different ways. Salespeople are often excited about new additions and expanding range but get confused when two plus two becomes three or even worse two, Sometimes adding products doesn't drive the changes you or your sales team wanted.

Clearly different products, even when sold to the same customer, using similar buyer journeys may need an entirely different SalesDISK©s.

Sadly, adding products or handling variations is where most companies do poorly and for many line extensions they cannibalise or die out due to lack of interest. The normal failure is releasing without modifying your sales plan and expecting organic take up by both sales and your customers.

*Channel Appropriate*

Are your products correct for your channel?
Can the value of your product be explained by a distributor? If it's too complex or used in too complicated a situation this can become hard for a distributor who is more likely to be selling your product as one of many. Distributors are normally selected based on the markets they already serve and the domain knowledge that comes with them.
If the distributor has access but not skill, then you may need to help them with demonstrations and application discussions. I have watched so many people (myself included) set up distribution, expecting them to be able to handle products but ending up needing to help. As a dealer manager in these situations, you end up visiting a region and then being chauffeured around to meet customers. This is fine as long as it's in the plan and you've decided this is the relationship you will have. Of course, there are other ways this can work and sometimes you just get lucky due to a key person.

*New Products*

Adding new products requires real skill, products normally come in two forms, product line extensions or new products which perform new jobs. When selling product line extensions, sometimes these will be above your solution and help expand applications or throughput; sometimes they will be below and used to address different price points or subtly different markets.
Salespeople that are hitting target/quota with your existing product will find it hard to swap customers to new products based on the risk of destroying their own commission. One theory I was presented with recently was where salespeople on lower base-to-commission ratios will take more risks because you're paying. If you're asking them to put their large commission at risk by trying new things, then they are less likely to try for you - and you won't fire them because they are still winning. I like this theory and wish I'd known it 20 years ago - for a start it could have helped me up my base salary.
If you're adding products to new markets, then again you're introducing risk for your sales staff. These sales staff can either be employed (direct sales) or dealers. In each case you need to try and

reduce the risk in some way. You may also need new dealers because, as noted previously, you selected them to serve specific markets, if you change the market the new products are to be sold into, then the dealer's value drops. Of course, this is harder where people have set up exclusive agreements, which I've found are to be avoided.

If you're adding new products you may need to consider new SalesDISK©s entirely and with new salespeople/channels to cover them. This can of course be costly and will be a function of the opportunity available and if there is capacity in the existing salesperson. If they are already at their transactional limit, you may be forced to add new people regardless.

*Sales Model Value Proposition*

How you set the expectations of your products value with your customer will drive the focus of your SalesDISK©. Imagine having a high-value luxury product such as a super yacht. The expectation that I think we all have is that it's a luxurious process; you would not expect to be welcomed aboard your "demo" with coffee in a plastic cup, this is champagne time - time to see how your life will be after you own the boat. I also imagine that there is a lot of configuration, one hot tub or two for example. I expect the DEVELOP and SERVICE segments to feature highly. I wouldn't expect them to spend ages cold-calling billionaires so the IDENTIFY segment is probably minimised.

Now consider buying a stereo system, there are some very high-end stores which will allow you to come in, try various records and speaker combinations. That's their experience - alternatively Amazon will deliver your goods tomorrow.

What do your product lend themselves to? Do you want to give a demonstration and installation experience using what my friend Jeff would call the white glove experience?

Are you designing a beautiful sale with an experience or just an easy transaction?

In the book, The Discipline of Market Leaders by Michael Treacy and Fred Wiersema, they propose that businesses work best when they adopt and exploit a value discipline to help drive the business and make hard decisions faced when you need to spend scarce resource.

As leaders you are going to face these decisions all the time as you can't say yes to everything asked of you - adding a machine to the production line to reduce lead time and lower costs versus adding a marketing campaign to grow business in China. Every day the leadership team and ultimately the leader has to make calls. Having and knowing a value discipline helps make the decision and defend it.

The book lays out the case with examples that there are 3 value disciplines Product Leadership, Operational Excellence and Customer Intimacy. It is important to note that these are value disciplines which shape the organisations, culture, management, core processes and IT structure. They are not 100% focused on how to sell a product. However, I actually think it lends itself nicely for considering how to set out your sales value.

The best way to consider this is to think about how customers make their decisions to purchase – we are complicated beasts and so we can use differing criteria for different categories.

Here are 3 examples from my life relating to my wardrobe:

*Product Leadership - Shoes*

Churches are a British shoe manufacturer established in 1873; their shoes are handmade in a factory in Northampton. They are the best. In my mind there is no question of this.

When I was 13, I was hit by a car. Thankfully I was ok but the arch ligaments in my feet were torn, and I had hours of physiotherapy. Like most teenagers I did not do all the exercises I should, so I have flat feet, my feet now eat shoes, destroying them within months. Churches' are $500 and they are worth it. As Tim who featured in chapter one would say "Spend a lot of money on your bed or your boots as if you're not in one you're in the other!".

I decided I must have the best; they are the best.

*Customer Intimacy – Suits & Shirts*

TM Lewin and Sons operate from the famous Jermyn Street in London. They have stores across the United Kingdom selling a range of formal business attire. Suits and shirts are obviously available in every department store across the UK, in more convenient settings, at cheaper prices and probably of equivalent quality, but I selected TM

Lewin - why? TM Lewin's is simply focused on everyday professional office wear, and they staff it to serve customers seeking assistance.

The business can sometimes be seen as a stock market for shirts with bundle sales fluctuating as its main promotion. Each day it appears they have a new deal 3 for $100 one day or 4 for $110. This concept of a deal is fine, it can be a value owned by the business, I know I can get 3 shirts for $100 - it's the fluctuation of the deals I find annoying.

The real thing I enjoy about TM Lewin's is the people who work there are trained to help exactly me. They make recommendations, measure, help, advise and service. They are not simply staff to restock shelves and work the tills, they employ skill.

In 2018 after two decades of gradually adding weight I decided enough was enough and lost 25kg (50 lbs US) I had to purchase an entire new wardrobe and so went to TM Lewin. As I walked through the door I was immediately asked by the assistant if they could help. Normally I would say "no thanks, just looking', but this time I said "yes I travel to Tokyo on Monday for a week of meetings. I need a new suit, shirt, belt etc, and I'm completely out of my depth." I was given fantastic personal service by a team who went above and beyond. It was like being in Pretty Woman!

*Operational Excellence – Gap Inc.*

GAP is a machine, a repetitive machine. Unlike TM Lewin's, I will get no advice, I get asked if anyone can help me, but this is normally just looking for sizes. That part of their model has failed or simply been abandoned. What they do is T-Shirts, Hoodies, and Sweatshirts.

I get exactly what I want, it's easy and I like it. It is not the best, it is not best service, it's just cheap, easy, and fine.

In fact, I've decided that a black or white T-Shirt needs no speciality from a product point of view, and I need no exceptional service. I just need extra small (check me out - I used to be a medium!). I want cheap and repeatable.

As I write, GAP has made the decision to close 81 stores in the UK and notes it will sell off its stores in France and Italy, moving online. Does this mean Operational Excellence failed for Gap? There are a number of reasons why but a big one is they were outperformed by companies doing the same thing. In the UK one main retailer was better at the job of cheap and that was Primark. Then there is the internet and the large number or players who can compete there using the same value set.

In fact, closing stores is not a failure it may even be considered as the ultimate move towards Operational Excellence. I will keep buying online - I know the brand, we have a relationship. Only time will tell. I say only time will tell because every book I read from 15-20 years ago slates Apple. I've looked into it, they did ok.

The three value disciplines can be viewed from the customer point of view in figure 10.2.

| | COST | BENEFIT |
|---|---|---|
| PRODUCTS | BEST TOTAL COST "Great Prices & Quality" "Their products last and last and last" "A no hassle firm" "Consistency is their name" | BEST PRODUCT "Premium product, but with it" "Customers ask for it by name" |
| SERVICES | | BEST TOTAL SOLUTION "They are experts in my business" "Their services are exactly what I need" |

Figure 10.2 – Value disciplines from customer view ("The Discipline of Market Leaders" by Michael Treacy and Fred Wiersema)

Customers segment products into 3 categories best price, best product and best total solution, matching how you design your sales model will need to reflect this. You can't position yourself as the "best product" without a sales model to match and enforce that position. In the same way that you can't say you're experts without meetings and discussions or be best value and then add lots of complication to the sale or service provided.

Customer intimacy businesses may want less time prospecting, (IDENTIFY segment), and give more attention to the heart of solving the customers solution – maximising the DEVELOP and KNOWLEDGE segments.

Operational excellence businesses may want to maximise the SERVICE segment, minimising the KNOWLEDGE segment. It is common to want to make the transaction as simple as possible and so they may wish to minimise sales input; here a better website or videos showing capability may reduce the need for the DEVELOP segment while also demonstrating KNOWEDLGE. With the emergence of more globalised markets, as discussed in the previous chapter, these web businesses are now more possible especially with lower ASP (average sale price) or highly specialised or niche products.

Product innovation-focused businesses often have to focus on the product value to justify higher margins so they may want to spend more on the KNOWLEDGE segment to help position the sale. If the technology is not mainstream and already adopted, more time may have to be spent finding the customers or proving the concept – expanding the IDENTIFY and DEVELOP segments.

Having a solid and visible sales value helps drive differences between you and your competitors helping customers position your company. It's not always easy but explaining how you do business and owning the position is a good thing to do. It's better to drive real wedges than to have the customer separate you from your competitors based on your colour scheme.

Although I point this out to help build sales strategy, the value discipline runs deeper and should set the value for your entire business. In one business I was involved in it was a key part of our recovery, and the simple act of picking a discipline gave us a mechanism of making future investment decisions. I say "simple act of picking a discipline" – 3 days locked in a meeting room debating it amongst the management team was not pleasant. It was highly emotional and at times strayed from the professional, but it was the correct thing to do.

We picked product leadership. With this the marketing and engineering teams drove new product design and when the new "best" product came out, we were ready with three separate SalesDISK©s. One for our entry-level products, one for our high-end and one for OEM. They were so varied we needed 3 separate sales teams.

With our entry level products, we stripped out KNOWLEDGE almost completely. We designated these products as commodities that were to be sold quickly and with less fuss-and-show than our high-end. We used fresh, relatively low-cost graduates to service leads only, reducing the focus on the IDENTIFY segment. We put everything into the DEVELOP and SERVICE segments. Critically the SalesDISK© was small. We needed the resource to push other opportunities. The low-cost graduates got what they wanted; it wasn't all one way. They were supported, educated, and helped to develop into higher level positions. Our focus was to feed the high-end, end-user business. We wanted adoption and, critically, by KOLs (key opinion leaders). We pushed heavily on IDENTIFY and DEVELOP segments, our mission was simple. Show the new technology and drag as many people through as possible. For the next few years this was the main SalesDISK© and main mission.

We spent time cautiously managing the KNOWLEDGE segment; growing it - not in sales but by building an affordable applications team. This also strengthened the DEVELOP segment where we made a more efficient demonstration process.

The actions of the high-end end-user products got the attention of the OEM customers, who we strongly believe may have done better under a customer intimacy model. However, they were happy to forgo intimacy to access new capabilities for their next generation instruments. We were now more about "what more could you do to make a better solution for your customers" than a simple replacement option based on price or to fix dissatisfaction with their current vendor. The OEM SalesDISK© remained medium in size, with its efforts following those of the end-user business. We still needed to focus on the IDENTIFY and DEVELOP segments to get the technology positioned for longevity.

We started by adding more prospecting resource to work on new methods such as LinkedIn Sales Navigator - long established but new to us. When a long-standing intimacy legend in our business retired, they were replaced with a person more in line with an IDENTIFY segment mind-set. We continued to invest and added more people to this team, growing it and its revenues. If it has not already done so, OEM revenue will soon overtake and surpass the end-user business.

Having and agreeing a value discipline added direction to our business. It shaped our decision making and helped drive the focus in sales & marketing.

## CHAPTER SUMMARY

How complicated your product is or how complicated the job it performs is, will determine how you plan on selling and demonstrating its value.

Customers often confuse solutions and commodities. If your product has real value, it needs to be positioned as and sold as a solution.

Niche products, especially those in new markets will need high knowledge to explain and position value and will need strong IDENTIFY segment to find the customers.

Distributor channels often provide coverage by existing in your target markets but may not always be capable of owning the value of your products and demonstrating them.

Adding new products may make you consider whether new channels or salespeople should be deployed. You may be increasing the risk for successful salespeople and so you may not achieve traction. The risk must be reduced and may need new salespeople and SalesDISK©s.

What is your sales value proposition? How are you telling customers you do business and with what product value?

Value disciplines are product leadership (best product) customer intimacy (best solution) and operational excellence (best total cost).

# Chapter 11: Customers

- Can I segment my customers?
- Can I build audiences?
- How do customers buy?
- What channels should I use?

*Segments, Profiles, Personas and Audiences*

How you form your SalesDISK© will depend on the customers you choose to serve in your markets. That is right I said choose to serve - most of us have faced tough times, when any customer with any interest will do, but you should at least start off with a plan to serve a type of customer.

Customer segmentation is an incredibly important tool to help focus marketing and sales efforts. In its most basic form, you can segment on age, sex, location. When I was a young rep in my early 20s, I preferred, and so targeted, customers who were older and more established in their positions - for me they were professors rather than doctors. Selling into academic research, I found that youth favoured "whistles and bells" and the older cohort favoured solutions to problems and good service. They valued the SERVICE segment, wanted relationships and for me to turn up on time and do what I said I was going to do. In return they were loyal and repetitive.

We all exist in segments designed by companies targeting us. As an example, I consistently would get hit with targeted messages in LinkedIn - why? Because they knew my title (vice president), organisation size (many hundreds), and location (UK), and so could estimate my buying power, interests, and authority.

Segments are essential for audience building, just like the people targeting me; if I can build a segment, I can build an audience. If I have an audience, I can understand where to place messages that will resonate with them. The audience can be known or presumed. A known audience can be a list of previously interested customers, people who attended a trade show, webinar, a purchased list etc. Critically, it has to be written down in a way that enables a sales or marketing person to communicate with them. For example, "we spoke to you at the World of Widgets trade show in 2019, are you still doing....."

Within segments will be profiles and personas which are often confused, frequently by myself. Profiles are based on existing customer interactions, whereas personas are based on ideal customers.

Profiles help marketing to map out jobs to be done and are developed by interactions. Much of the investigation into profile is done through voice-of-customer interviews conducted by marketing. These profiles help to shape not only the input of product development, but to help position existing features and benefits - helping sales and marketing messaging.

I highly recommend any book on job theory, anything which explores the job to be done by the consumer. The concept is simple, if you understand the job to be done, you can design products to do that job better, sometimes making it easier or sometimes improving what Adrian J Slywotzky, in his book "Demand", calls the Hassle Map.

In "What Customers Want" by Anthony W Ulwick, he explores the idea that what a customer wants never gets explained by the customer. They are not experienced in product design; they only can work on minor improvements to existing products declaring where they may be better or picking pure fantasy answers such as I just want to close the lid and have it do everything. The classic quote here is of course Henry Ford's "If I asked people what they wanted they would have said faster horses."

Ulwick proposes that by looking at each step of a job to be done you can look for improvements, some of which can make the job significantly easier. Real world examples of this are all around us. Why on earth do we need tablets - we have laptops? Touch screen and removal of the keyboard made it more like a magazine and a more enjoyable experience to surf. Why e-readers over tablets? High gloss reflective displays of tablets made it hard to read outside on vacation next to the pool.

What I have always found overlooked is that the voice-of-customer work, which is normally done pre-release, should continue past the release of the product. Customers truly help identify sales and marketing points you might never had thought of through their deep use. I have in my time re-launched products based on customer feedback on points we felt had little or no value at the time of launch – later learning customers loved them.

Where profiles help drive voice-of-customer, personas are fictional customers who help marketing teams construct messages that will resonate. I used personas with salespeople to help them classify customers and get them to understand their position and thoughts.

Personas are great fun. As an example, one of my companies used to sell to customers at universities, mainly to physics and biology labs. We had a customer segment we defined as homebuilder. This segment assembled solutions from parts rather than buying completed solutions from instrument companies. They were cutting edge, many of them were designing new instruments or looking for improvements in existing. Within this segment was a persona we had created who we called 'Richard the post-doc', and we could dive so deep into the persona we could even identify their clothes.

One day I was waiting, with a new salesperson, for a customer in a reception area of a building at Stanford University, all I knew was we were meeting someone called Matthew. I predicted the Matthew would be wearing cargo pants, sneakers (not Nike probably Adidas or Vans). They would have a t-shirt or check shirt. If a t-shirt, it would not be plain but would have a large image filling the front, and there was a greater than 50% chance he'd have a beard. I was bang on the money. Why? Because I had studied the persona a lot and also had history having met a lot of people like him.

The best salespeople I've ever met are empathetic and understand all aspects of their customers' needs and wants whether they are application, business or personal.

Creating personas with experienced people in the room is easy. Simply get a large piece of paper and draw a stick person, give them a name (Susan, Brian and Alan are my go-to examples) and write notes surrounding them about what you think they care about for certain things, what gets in their way, how do your products feature in their busy lives.

I believe empathy is the single largest tool for selling, this is one of the major reasons I like the STRONGMAN sales methodology by Ed Wal, as it puts all the analysis on the deal from the prospect's point of view.

Once we know our customers through either recording voice-of-customer from profiles or by building personas, we can look at the way they buy.

What motivates your customers to contact you? How do you prove your solution is valid? How do they like to finally place the order?

*Buyer Journey*

It is estimated an average adult makes 35,000 remotely conscious decisions a day. You are a decision-making machine. Some of these decisions are purchases, some high-speed and some complex well thought out. How buyers make purchasing decisions can be distilled into what is known as the buyer journey.

The buyer journey looks at the sale entirely empathetically from the buyer's point of view. By understanding it we can design, market to, and sell to the buyer with greater impact.

Some customers want a transaction (immediate satisfaction), some want a consultant (speak to an expert), and some want to join an eco-system (I want to join your club and way of interacting).

Although buyers tend to follow a standard buyer journey, they can often feel very different because of the speed travelled, stages jumped and even reverses. As an example, buying a coffee and a house follow similar processes but I have never spent 6 months going backwards and forwards when buying a coffee. However, the structure of the journey, when distilled, was actually very similar.

At its heart is the basic structure of the buyer journey

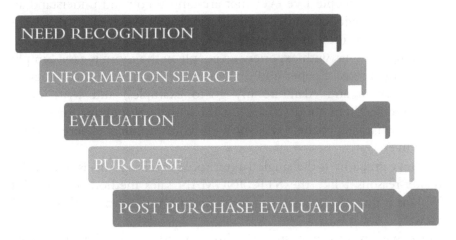

NEED RECOGNITION

INFORMATION SEARCH

EVALUATION

PURCHASE

POST PURCHASE EVALUATION

Figure 11.1 - Classic buyer journey

Let's just consider the overall concept with that coffee purchase.

- Need recognition. I'm tired and thirsty I need a coffee
- Information search. Is there a coffee shop around here?
- Evaluation. It's Starbucks, I like Starbucks, I've had it before
- Purchase. Stand in line, "Large coffee please"
- Post purchase evaluation. I feel fuller, more alert now let's get on

Simple isn't it. You are probably thinking well what did that tell me? I remember there were a lot more conversations, meetings, quoting, demos, etc when I did my last sale.

Part of the reason it may not have clicked with you yet is you need to see it from the buyer's position and not yours. Your task is to understand how they purchase and try to best match this with your sales model as is represented by your SalesDISK©.

*Need Recognition*

Need recognition sounds a bit like someone having an epiphany, Oh I need …. However, for many things life is not like this, needs come and go. Some days I'm ready to buy a new iPad because I convince myself I need one, then I calm down. I often think I need new golf clubs but surely my existing 5-year-old set can't be that bad - they work (sort of), why am I even considering it? I don't need them, or do I?

This thought process is nicely explained by Maslow's hierarchy of needs.

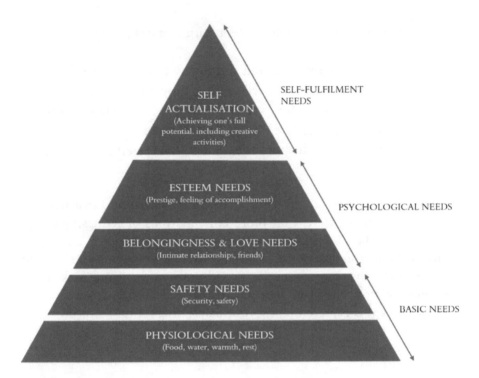

Figure 11.2 – Maslow's hierarchy of needs

In 1943 Abraham Maslow proposed that needs could be separated into basic needs (physiological and safety), psychological needs (belongingness and esteem) and finally self-actualisation needs (being the best you can be). In recent years, memes have added Wi-Fi and battery life at the bottom, below basic needs.

Most people we know have basic needs covered (sadly not all), but we can see that above basic needs is where my new golf clubs come in and why I drive a car with a logo on, for which I am aligned to the company brand values. Basically, I want to be in that gang, tribe, group etc.

Earlier in the book I recalled the story of my visit to TM Lewin & Sons where the sales assistant asked if I needed help and I said, "I travel to Tokyo on Monday for a week of meetings, I need a new suit, shirt, belt etc, and I'm completely out of my depth."

So, my need was specifically a suit 38" chest, shirt 15" neck, belt 30". No, my need was to look professional, gain the respect of others and look good. Clothes were just a mechanism to get me there. We had just successfully sold the business and I was meeting the local managers of the parent company and their distribution network; psychological needs were my motivator.

In "Solution Selling, the Strongman Process" by Ed Wal, he proposes that there are 3 types of needs to consider during a purchase - application, business and personal.

Figure 11.3 – Composition of application, business & personal needs

I prefer this when assessing a sale or purchase as it considers the personal, as Maslow explains, and adds in the business (organisation or entity) and applicational (specific solution sought) needs.

So, we can see that there are different needs but where do the needs come from?

Needs can be self-diagnosed or developed. Self-diagnosed needs can be as simple as replacing broken or old, if you have a flat tyre, your need is immediate - you can immediately self-diagnose that you need a patch or a new tyre.

In my personal life, most of my needs are self-diagnosed and based on replace/repair or ego-based progression - want bigger house, better car, etc. Within business I can self-diagnose other needs to fix existing or expected problems, or to take advantage of opportunities such as needing replication, scale, or progression.

Company diagnosed needs, a form of self-diagnosed needs, are where a group of people have decided a problem exists that needs to be fixed - sometimes because of kaizen, and sometimes because of pain being felt. For example, we need to review service - it's a companywide problem. Sometimes it can even be that purchasing have diagnosed: 'we no longer trust supplier X, they have been late and of poor quality and we need this vendor replaced'.

Developed needs I would best explain as needs which would never have occurred unless presented as a problem. Clearly buyers need to be aware of solutions, if you have a flat tyre the chances are you know where your local tyre place is and how to get it fixed. This is awareness and is controlled mainly by marketing, however sales and sales coverage can play a very strong part in making people aware.

There are some developed needs which are a little different – they are needs which are identified by salespeople through discussion. At its most basic level, if you call an existing buyer with a 10-year-old product, chances are you can discuss with them what they do and understand their jobs, not needs, and then you can start to develop needs.

I'm very strict here – discuss with them their jobs, not needs. At this point in time the buyers' needs relative to their position are met. They have a solution - it works, thanks. Only after discussing their jobs and jobs of similar example, buyers can you develop a need and get them to recognise it.

You purchased the CoolMatic4500 nice, what do you use it for? How do you set it up? How long does that take? That sounds annoying – did you know the CoolMatic5000 does that in a few seconds making the task 100x faster.

In "Competing Against Luck", Clayton M. Christianson proposes that products or services are simply hired to do jobs. If they do them well, they get rehired. If they do them badly, they get fired.

When developing needs, you are asking the buyer to fire their current solution and hire yours because it does the job better. You are developing and attempting to satisfy that need.

Just as with self-diagnosed, developed needs are pushed through marketing messages and then distributed through marketing channels such as print adverts, trade shows, social media content, talks, articles, etc. For example, "CoolMatic5000 the fastest solution for Coolflip development - up to 100x faster than other solutions."

These messages sometimes just don't get through - why? Maybe you're too niche, too new, too unknown. Maybe your message is just not compelling enough, or simply your communication channels fail. In these situations the developed needs are best created by a sales team with a large IDENTIFY segment focus which is sometimes married to a high KNOWLEDGE segment.

If you can get a salesperson to talk on the phone to a prospect in a clear segment, then they can discuss their situation, jobs to be done and start to develop needs.

Existing customer lists are a great place to start. With a product older than 10 years, the customer may be thinking of replacing it at some point. If 10% of people replace (fire) their solution every 10 years, then give me 100 customers and I will give you 10 projects. Remember it could be 10 years or 12. We just hope it wasn't 8 years and they never called because the only thing you had at the time was the CoolMatic4500 and that had the long set-up time.

It doesn't have to just be existing customers (farming), it can be your competitors' customers, people doing the job with another tool – basically any group of people that you can segment and achieve a reasonable match with (prospecting).

Finally, please be hyper aware that needs compete. You are more likely to lose any proposed solution to something completely different. My nice new Cobra golf clubs may lose to TaylorMade but they are more likely to lose to a watch, fancy dinner or part of the designer kitchen living in my wife's mind!

In "Solution Selling, The STRONGMAN Process" Ed Wal proposes that the options for the buyer are as below.

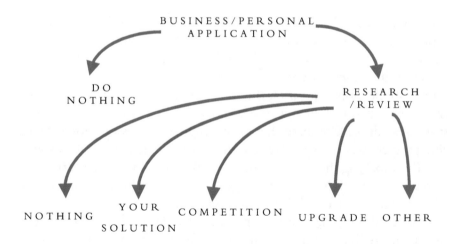

Figure 11.4 – Buyer options

During need identification, the prospect can choose to do nothing or move to research or review and from here they have several paths to conclusion.

During the early section of the sale, if you ask a salesperson what the prospects options are, they will probably tell you a competitor's name, even if they are not involved in the slightest. They will rarely tell you one of the other outcomes. In sales, doing nothing or other is the largest reason leads don't progress. Unless there is a rock-solid need such as replace broken or expand capability/capacity - I can't fix a flat tyre with much else other than a new tyre.

This is at the core of why many businesses set up sales teams to service marketing leads. It's a lot easier for sales to service leads than to create opportunities themselves. However, for some businesses, depending on the situation, it is an absolute must. This could be because you're launching, you need to push beyond serviced leads expectations, or because you're in survival-mode. I've lived all three.

Marketing, during the need recognition stage, should be creating awareness of your solution through placing your messages in the correct places for the correct audiences. Tactics are normally social media content, trade shows, email programs, training or educational events.

*Information Search*

As soon as a need has been recognised the next step is for the buyer to rank their need and then move into research or review. Research can be considered as noncritical and searching for possible options whereas review is investigating with clear purpose.

Think about shopping for clothes, for me in TM Lewin, I was clearly in review - it was their suit or a suit from the John Lewis department store next door. Compare this to the endless hordes of people filling shopping centres on Saturdays looking for inspiration or deals. I sound like I'm mocking these people but for golf clubs, I'm in the early stage of research myself. My friend just got a new driver from Cobra, I have tried it and it's on a wish list in my head somewhere.

To make sales that convert happen salespeople need to be talking to buyers in review, and they need to filter out those in research. Prospects in research can purchase by rapidly being moved into review. This requires a problem to arise which accelerates their need, for example someone stole my golf clubs and I play on Sunday. Alternatively, if the sticker shock is so large, I can be persuaded to overtake competing needs, 30% off Cobra drivers one day only - sorry darling, the kitchen can wait.

People get very confused when they compare tradeshow lead conversion rate with website leads, but it's simple - buyers visit tradeshows either before need awareness or in a very passive information search (research). These are not bad leads - they are just very early leads, possibly several years off; you need to service these leads but do so with less vigour than leads which are in review. Website leads are normally more of an investment for the buyer with more hoops to jump through, they have consciously started reading material and then completing a form asking for contact.

At this stage the buyer is most likely going to start with the logical basics just as you would, you are a buyer by the way. Web searches, review of known brands, talking to friends and colleagues and vendor engagement.

During information search, marketing is focused on SEO, Google Ads, selection tools, messages, social game, and brand. Buyers are effectively standing outside our store looking in and wondering if they should go in and try on our products for fit. In fact, that's our main threat - the buyer is looking to qualify us in or out, they want to narrow their search.

So, where are sales in this step? What can your people do here? Well first thing is to respond - it's amazing how bad some sales organisations or salespeople can be at responding.

Not responding to a lead or request for information is a sure-fire way to get qualified out early. The first experience you have with a company can forge the relationship you have with them for life. For example, when I was 23, I was given a car allowance from work, I went to look at cars at the local Audi dealership, they were dismissive and uninterested - I will never buy an Audi. That was my experience. Audi are good - they probably have millions of happy buyers I'm sure, but the link in my brain has been created and it will be hard to break it without a monumental reason.

What information does the buyer want? Well normally pricing, they are looking initially to qualify you out, but they still want to discuss if it's the correct product, configuration and may even want to know more about demonstrating capability through things such as references.

Remember, your aim is to get the buyer to evaluation. Your strategy may be to give away all information so they can self-serve. Alternatively, it may be to withhold key information ensuring further contact. As an example, if you list prices, you may be qualified out before being able to explain your value. You could equally argue that you might filter out timewasters who could never spend at the correct level.

You can use tools to watch how your buyers travel through your website and where they jump off, possibly giving up or possibly satisfied. With cookie-tracking and smart marketing tools, you can even see when buyers are returning for more information and send alerts to sales to follow up. I love technology like this. I also urge caution when deploying it, as sometimes your salespeople don't need the distractions. These can work but, like everything, you need execution. I've seen people implement them and do nothing or just talk a great game but never get around to implementing.

Conversion rates from website visits to completed lead forms can be as low as 0.1% and up to around 2%. We once had a problem with page conversions on the contact us page - you would hope that 80% of people who reached this page would enter their details but for some reason we we're only achieving about 10%. In the end we discovered the endless questions asked turned people off and they gave up. From then on, we only asked for, name, organisation, country, phone, email and what they wanted to know from us.

*Evaluation*

The evaluation is complex; part of it will of course be the demonstration of capability but there are a lot of possible actions being completed by the buyer at this point.

The buyer is consciously or subconsciously, writing a pros and cons list. They are also probably bringing more people into the decision, asking for external feedback and possibly even reconsidering needs.

Salespeople are looking to demonstrate capability, identify and handling objections, position features and benefits, and in some cases re-engineering needs to better fit their suggested solution. Their job is to be constantly trying to control that pros-and-cons list, tilting it in their favour, whilst trying to create the comfort required for the next stage, purchase.

You are also now playing Battleships with your competitors. Battleships, for those of you born after 1990, is a game where each competitor sets up a series of plastic ships over a grid. Your opponent (competitor) can't see where your ships are, and you can't see theirs. Each player (vendor) takes it in turn to call out grid references relating to your opponent's set up. Your aim is to call a grid reference where they have placed a ship. You want to hit their ships before they hit yours.

What I'm trying to say is you are selling to the buyer, providing information, developing and re-engineering needs that match your product, the problem is so are your competitors, but you can't see what they are saying so don't know how to react.

Buyers give some things away, mainly as questions to your salesperson which are regurgitations of your competitors sticky benefit statements or perceived advantages for example, how important is millisecond timing and how do you account for variations? The salesperson thinks "wow, where did that come from". The other impact of this Battleship game is that your buyer is being constantly influenced up and down the buyer journey by competitors and other external world factors.

You could be in evaluation and then the buyer moves back to information search; you may think you are about to close when the buyer sees a post on social media from an ex-colleague noting that they love the new solution from company X, or they receive a 20% off promotional email from company Y who were originally qualified out. There are lots of things designed to change the buyer's positions within the buyer journey.

A thousand things can happen between now and receiving the purchase order - most of them are bad. That is why I recommend that salespeople with reasonable deal-sizes do weekly opportunity reviews with their managers. This is also why I have always used STRONGMAN© to review opportunities. It forced honesty and allowed us to see if we could win or if we should spend time looking for other deals.

If you expect that the battleground will be in evaluation, due to high rivalry amongst existing competitors, then you should maximise your efforts on the DEVELOP Segment of SalesDISK©

*Purchase*

In 2003 I was given a brand from a new business unit recently purchased by our parent group to run across the UK and shortly thereafter in Europe. The value discipline of the business was operational excellence, they made high value low-cost products, they were not the best, nor were they presented as such but they were easy. We lived one single rule with this brand as we launched it - make it ridiculously easy to do business with us and I mean ridiculously - we wanted zero hurdles. Everything was fast, easy, if we had an unsatisfied customer, we swapped out their product same day, we set hard expectations and we hit them.

Doing business with someone should be easy. Even if you're a big company with lots of different hoops to jump through, that is no excuse for not setting expectations and helping the buyer purchase your products.

Have you ever tried to buy something and it was just too hard? Many times I've walked into a busy Apple© store waving a credit card, saying I want to buy something while their sales assistants ignore me and continue to discuss features with interested unfunded teenagers and tech cautious octogenarians. I just want a cash register. I come back though, damn them, their stylish products and their exploitation of my psychological needs.

Purchase starts with the price, configuration and sometimes negotiation and ends when the buyer makes their decision and commitment to purchase.

In many sales this is easy enough for the buyer - just give me a quote, I will send it to the purchasing department to cut the order, or here is a credit card.

This can be further complicated for the buyer by required restrictions on sign-off and the formal-and-fair purchasing programs. Vendors may require the sign-off end-user statements for controlled goods or may want to dominate terms and conditions.

The buyer in most instances has purchased before and will know what to do. The seller should also know the procedure and should be there to help reduce friction.

As with evaluation the SalesDISK© DEVELOP segment is the key to winning if you perceive that purchasing and how orders are processed is a key factor.

No matter the scale and size of the purchase, buying should not be a pain. People do give up; sometimes even your product's compelling nature is overcome by the frustrations of doing business with you. I've walked away, backed out of a deal once commitment has been made - as have you, even if it's just leaving a non-moving line to get into a nightclub or bar.

*Post Purchase Evaluation*

After the buyer places their order, the goods arrive - maybe they need installation and training, maybe there is instant satisfaction or start-up teething issues. Once they use the product without you there, they become your customer. At some point, as a customer, they will evaluate their decision, again this is often subconscious only to be recalled on request. This evaluation will of course be for the product and the purchase experience.

As a real-world example, I just had a coffee, it was Nespresso, from a machine in my kitchen, I have not given my feedback to Nespresso but overall, it was good. Same could be true of my car, the purchase was several hundreds of thousands of times larger than the coffee but actually no one asked.

The car, a Land Rover (don't judge), is good by the way, and the experience of purchasing it was in fact pleasant. I liked the salesperson, he listened and came up with suggestions, he made me feel like we were a team solving my problem. Part of my problem was getting it in time and he jumped to get this sorted for me; he re-engineered my needs a little to get me there, but it was good. At the time he knew I was expecting a child and when I took delivery there were associated baby travel items - nice touch.

The salesperson did the handover, not a new person for me to meet but him. Really, he should have been working another deal with a new buyer, but their model built the relationship and kept the intimacy until the end. I would re-buy the brand from that dealer and ask for that salesperson again.

Sometimes skills, focus and efficiency mean that your salespeople can't be involved that heavily to do the handover. Sometimes basic economics, availability or relationship mean that you have chosen to use the salesperson to complete and manage the final stage of delivery and acceptance.

The job is now to make the customer become a fan, encouraging repeat purchase or simply helping encourage others. If possible, this can be done by sales or marketing, normally both.

The smart ones amongst you may have noticed that buyer journey seems to overlap with the SalesDISK© segments. Need identification and information search are directly linked to the SalesDISK© IDENTIFY segment. The evaluation and purchase steps within the buyer journey overlap directly with DEVELOP and post purchase evaluation overlaps with the SERVICE segment.

KNOWLEDGE does not overlap with any specific part of the buyer journey; it serves all and relates more to the complexities of the products and their use.

| BUYER JOURNEY STAGE | CUSTOMER STATE | SALESDISK© SEGMENT |
|---|---|---|
| Need Recognition | Happy/Content or Annoyed/Troubled | IDENTIFY |
| Information Search | Review or Research | IDENTIFY |
| Evaluate | Review or Research | DEVELOP |
| Purchase | Negotiating/Buying | DEVELOP |
| Post Purchase Evaluation | Deployment/Assessment | SERVICE |

Figure 11.5 Buyer Journey relationship with SalesDISK© segment

*Channel*

Go-to-Market is not route-to-market. Products get to end-users through channels. Yes, you need to manage these channels and part of that relationship is selling but they should be considered channels, not customers.

People at this point will often tell me 'no my dealer is my customer'. This is partly true because they buy things from you and so a transaction occurred. Just remember that the transaction would not have occurred if it wasn't for another person's need, and that person was your customer. By all means, be nice to them, persuade them, present to them, treat them as a customer but just remember they are channels.

Channels can be considered any route to the end-user customer. Normally our brain divides channel into 2 choices direct or dealer. Direct being our own sales team that we believe we can drive at will and dealer being a partner who we outsource the task of sales and sometimes service to.

This is really important to remember. You have dealers so that you don't bear the operational costs in their territory. In most instances it is a like-for-like swap. If you sell $1M in that region and give the dealer a 25% discount, your direct alternative is spending $250,000 on a salesperson, their office, and all other infrastructure costs. You are probably going to want at least $2M or $3M to reach a worthy profit, after all the local and management costs are considered just to add one member of staff, and even then, are they going to cover as much ground as a dealer with multiple reps?

There is an exception to this like-for-like swap and that's if integration is required or they sell with other useful components. If a dealer adds your product to another and makes a solution, you now need a distributor or to allow your salesperson to copy, by adding 3rd party to their portfolio. This creates our 3rd category – value added resellers. For many years I assumed I had dealers. I was wrong I had value added resellers. When you have a VAR, your product is no longer sold as your product, and you become a component.

Dealers tend to be reactive and carry large portfolios, this is how they make money; they know if they carry enough product and see enough people they will sell enough stuff. Most don't directly replace the efforts of a direct salesperson -please don't expect them to without a really good opportunity to make them money.

Dealers typically get 20-30% discount on a product and need to make money. You will hopefully be making significantly more, but you're paying for R&D and running factories. For them to add a single salesperson to be exclusive on your products they need to sell as much as one of your direct salespeople to cover their costs and make profit.

If you don't have people working exclusively on your products, then dealers are always going to be lower in the KNOWLEDGE and

DEVELOP segments. If your product is complex, then they will be unlikely to be able to demonstrate it.

What is really clear is the job of sales through a dealer can't exactly match the SalesDISK© you plan on using for a direct salesforce. There are realistically 2 SalesDISK©s - one for the dealer manager and one for the dealer. In most instances they are going to be servicing local marketing leads, maybe you're better to help them plan to find customers rather than trying to teach them to look and act exactly like your direct sales team. What is very important is that if you have a dealer this does not mean you wash your hands of responsibility for the region - you still need to market and you still need customer interactions, unless you're declaring that market a skim market and anything is considered better than nothing.

The next channel which many people may well consider direct is OEM sales. OEM sales is only separate from normal direct sales if your product can be purchased as a single unit to satisfy a need, but if all you do is provide components, then this is your direct sales team. If you do both, you're going to need different SalesDISK©s. Unlike a dealer, VARs and OEMs do not need their own disk - they create their own demand as they have created their own products. They do need management and to be kept happy so they don't leave for competitors but how they sell their solution is up to them.

*Multichannel Strategies*

As well as dealer, VAR, and OEM we can further segment direct sales into field, phone, and web sales.

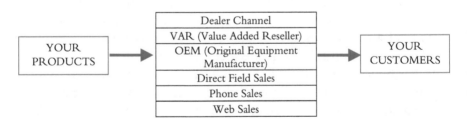

Figure 11.6 – Channels take your products to your customers

Multichannel strategies are common as people look to exploit opportunities, often serving high value opportunities directly and low value ones using phone or web sales. It may also be common to employ multiple dealers per market, which may of course cause conflict. Channel issues often occur when channels overlap, compete, and don't communicate. It is also worth noting that each channel is going to have a different cost and impact structure.

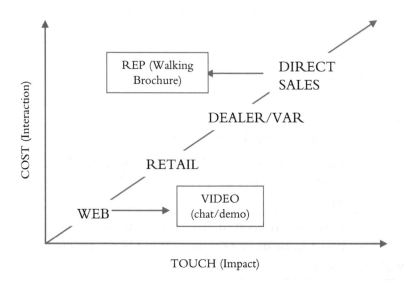

Figure 11.7 – Channel relative to cost per interaction and touch

In Figure 11.7 we can see, as expected, web is the lowest cost but least impact and direct sales are the highest cost and highest impact.

There are a couple of exceptions where the relationship breaks down. A positive is that video/chat functions, especially following forced adoption due to covid can increase touch relative to cost. The negative is that you can have sales reps that represent your business but actually don't create as much impact as true salespeople. Sometimes this is intentional but often it's down to poor definition.

## CHAPTER SUMMARY

People are making decisions constantly. When we look at how people buy, we can distil the process to what we call the buyer journey.

The buyer journey is made up of need recognition, information search, evaluation, purchase and post purchase evaluation.

Maslow's hierarchy of needs explains differing types of needs, the most basic being food, water and safety moving on to more complex psychological needs.

Within a purchase or sale, there are 3 groups of needs, application, organisational and personal.

Needs can be self-diagnosed or developed. Developed needs are established through the discussion of jobs being conducted by the prospect.

If the sales team are needed to drive demand, then a large emphasis needs to be placed on the IDENTIFY segment within SalesDISK©.

Your organisation needs to establish what information your buyers will seek during the information search phase and who will be responsible for responding to inbound requests.

Evaluation can comprise many things. It can be considered the pros-and-cons list which is either consciously or sub-consciously recorded.

Purchasing products should be low friction. No matter how big or complex you are, you can help a buyer through the purchasing process.

Depending on the need and constraints, salespeople can be used to help conclude the sale with installation and post-sales support.

The buyer journey overlaps with the SalesDISK© in certain areas, need identification and information search with

IDENTIFY, evaluation and purchase with DEVELOP and post purchase evaluation with SERVICE.

KNOWLEDGE has no overlap; it services all parts of the buyer journey, and its importance will depend on the complexity of the products and their use.

Customers are end-users. Any intermediary party in the process can be considered a channel, irrespective of whether a transaction occurred.

Channels are sometimes traded (direct for dealer) but there is always a trade-off and you will need dealer management with their own SalesDISK© to keep focus.

Channels vary in cost and impact. Many companies chose to operate multiple channels to achieve greater coverage.

# Chapter 12: Understanding Problems & Opportunities

Knowing the composition of your SalesDISK© means that you understand your problems and opportunities and are maximising your sales plan to drive impact. However, understanding your problems and opportunities is actually quite a hard thing to do.

People describe problems using symptoms such as "not winning enough deals" or "low pipeline". Problems are in fact a bit easier to work with than opportunities. Ask a salesperson what are their problems and they will talk for hours; ask them their opportunities to grow and they tend to struggle. Here you normally get a definition of a new product - one which is like the one they just lost to but a bit better. Or it could be needs, such as better support or more marketing. Salespeople tend to take route-one obviously which is fine and to be expected. They have their tasks and you, as a leader, have yours. They can help with feedback and ideas but you must own the growth.

We all struggle with opportunities for growth. We know that we have great products; we know that they are as good if not better than our competitors', but we stumble at what to do to connect these products to the prospects.

When we do think, then ideas start to come - this is excellent and exciting. But now, just like an investor, you need to work out where to put your money.

Many years ago, the business unit I was working with made money for the first time in a few years - it made a return of 5%. This was announced at the global sales meeting. We'd all flown in from around the world, we felt proud, happy, and successful. Then came the talk from the corporate divisional leader, he thanked us for our efforts and then asked for more. We of course felt exhausted and had no idea where to go, how could we do better?

His angle was simple. "You've made 5%. What was our alternative to having you do this work? Well, we could have taken the money, put it in a government bond, sat in a hot tub, smoked cigars, not listened to your struggles, and got the same result."

This was crushing - soul destroying even - but he was correct. Why work ourselves to the bone for 5% profit? Why not do smarter things? It took me many years to realise that he was correct. Everyone has choices of where to invest; everything has an opportunity cost.

**185**

Choosing to invest your time and money in one thing rather than another is really hard. Worse than that is continuing to march forward without tackling the need to make changes to stop the continual hand-to-mouth grind. This to me is why opportunities are much harder to understand than problems are to fix. Problems need isolating and fixing, opportunities need discovering, ranking, and investing.

Most companies have both problems and opportunities. Problems tend to show up as short-term. For example, we are going to miss revenue this quarter as the pipeline is too low. Opportunities tend to provide growth and also longer-term solutions to the problems.

Problems by their nature can be either fixed, patched or lived with. A big problem will need most resources to be deployed to fix it, even putting other opportunity-driven initiatives on hold.

Big problems are a threat to the continuation along your chosen path. For example, we need funding now or we can't pay people past July; we need to hit target or face job cuts; our backer may sell us or merge us, which may be good or bad but definitely out of our control. Big problems stop you on your march to your planned outcome.

Smaller problems are bumps in the road - they hurt but not as much. Sometimes they can be explained easily. For example, the salesperson in Germany is not what we want; they won't prospect; they only want to service leads - which will limit growth. However, they know the products and we have bigger problems. This example shows that smaller problems, like opportunities, can be ranked, and critically they can be patched or lived with. We know that we have a problem – it's on the back burner while we fight fire A or invest in idea B.

For big problems, often short-term tactics are needed. For sales these can be as simple as forced prospecting actions, promotions, playing games with incentives, throwing money at advertising. Big problems, as you can imagine, cause big distractions but often need dealing with. For this reason, recurring problems really need to be addressed as the distractions become too much. For example, if the problem every quarter is low pipeline or a pipeline that can't meet quota/target or goal, then this really needs to be challenged.

To assess my recurring problems and opportunities, I use a model called PPH$^{SM}$. PPH$^{SM}$ stands for Product, Presence and Hit rate and it was developed by Frank Lynn & Associates Inc. I and many of my colleagues - along with countless others helped by Frank Lynn & Associates Inc, - use it to assess markets served, to look for gaps and places to grow. Please note that this section is my interpretation, viewed specifically from a sales point-of-view, I highly recommend reading the expanded white papers at www.franklynn.com or attending one of their, or their affiliates' courses.

PPH$^{SM}$ nicely shows the levers that exist within a business to increase market share. I appreciate that by now some people will be thinking that we want to carve a new-world throwaway market share and do our own thing. Well, that's just a matter of how you view your market. If Amazon defined their market for Kindle at launch as 'people that use e-readers' then they would not have bothered. If they defined it as 'people who read books' then it's the different story that it turned out to be.

People also tend to get cross about market share because they normally think it's an old value and that other metrics are more important. The normal excuse used for growing market share is economies of scale giving better profits. This can of course fail if you buy the market through discounting.

Regardless, market share composition allows us to look at what we as a business can control.

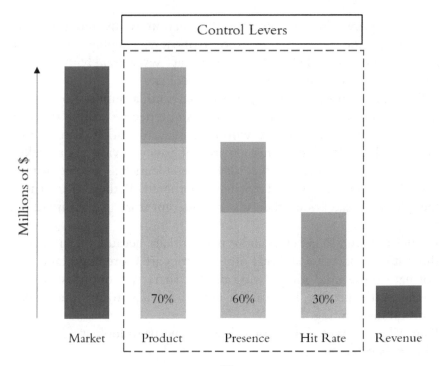

Figure 12.1 - A basic view of PPH$^{\text{SM}}$

The PPH$^{\text{SM}}$ model starts off with a market definition and an estimated market size value based on your definition. This will include any direct competitors to the product - normally companies that look like you. It also includes indirect competitors who don't look like you but can solve the customers' problem in a different way. This requires some thinking, but everything can be estimated by using a team of people and multiple inputs to drive an answer – sort of an educated wisdom of crowds concept.

After market comes product coverage. Based on the solutions in the market how much do your products cover through form, fit, function and pricing within 20%? For example, we have products X and Y. Our competitors have equivalents. However, we don't have product Z, and that accounts for 30% of the market revenue and so we address 70% of the market.

Next is presence, it is often the hardest leaver to calculate and so is commonly solved using the easier to determine product and hit rate values. Presence is made up by estimating how visible you are to customers (coverage) and how regularly you are quoted by your sales channel (offer rate).

This is hard, but for coverage I used to count competitive salespeople on trade show booths. Now I just count them on LinkedIn - thank you LinkedIn. For example, we have 10 salespeople in Europe. The competitors, collectively, have 30, so let's assume that I'm 25% covered. Now I could have a really efficient team who show up in most deals, so I could be 50% or even higher. This can be even seen in CRM reports where competitors are tracked. I've always found that in markets where there are 4 dominant players, you are normally in competition only with 2 of 3, as one has been discounted early on or was never selected. There are of course deals happening where people simply repeat without talking to competitors – this is all for you to model based on what you know.

Coverage is really key. It's amazing how much difference good coverage can make. You have to be in deals to win them and sometimes just showing up or having a dealer who can show up locally can have a massive effect.

Offer rate is a hard-to-swallow metric for managers. It's how often your product is shown and quoted. For direct sales teams this is normally as close to 100% as you can get. Some direct salespeople are efficient and know when they are losing and don't bid for things they know they will not win.

Distribution channels are much more interesting (or upsetting depending on your point of view). They also suffer from the "I'm not going to win this" factor seen with direct sales teams. This is amplified by the fact they don't have the same pressure to sell your product as your direct team do. They also have alternatives to sell which can get them to their quota - some directly competing in the same deals and some just taking more of their time way from focusing on you. Finally, they also have less KNOWLEDGE with which to defend deals so simply prefer to stay out or just not fight.

Hit rate - how many deals do I win? For this it's really about deals we played for and got - not lost deals that we didn't commit resources to or resulted in no transaction. This will normally be between 33% and 66%. If you're below 25% you're just quoting and hoping, and above 75% then there is not enough risk in your business and your salespeople are sitting in comfort zones.

Hit rate is where people tend to put energy into sales staff. They train salespeople to find and win deals, but actually there's a lot more to it. I'm not saying don't train salespeople - I think every salesperson should have an out-of-company sales mentor and coach who is working alongside your sales director. Your sales director is directing and setting standards - he isn't necessarily in charge or training. I am saying that sales staff are part of the hit rate problem but so are many other things. Maybe you need an easier sales process, better references – there are many reasons why you win or lose at the hit rate stage.

People often underestimate their hit rate when looking at CRM reports. This is mainly because they have not accounted for the impact of product and presence (coverage and offer rate). You may think 'well we lost that deal to Company X - we didn't chase' but remember, that's already accounted for in the offer rate. What about deals where we offered product A and they offered product B and we had no equivalent solution? Well, that's accounted for in product coverage. Ok last one, what about the guy in Boston who purchased from our competitor and we only found out about it after we saw it installed? Well, that was all about missing coverage.

Earlier on I said we often use the other data to calculate presence. This is because product managers should be able to do a good job of assessing product coverage and sales managers with CRM data can drive out reasonable hit rate data. With this information you can solve presence. To help with this assessment, Frank Lynn and Associates Inc. have some excellent calculators, and, as part of their consultancy, they or their associates can help guide you through the process.

Product coverage tactics can be as simple as new products, line extensions or as complicated as adding market changing services. Channel could be about new pricing strategies for dealers, changing your go-to-market, increasing marketing, brand building. Hit rate is of course sales training, but you could also drive through in product differentiation, references, key opinion leader programs, sales enablement tools. It's really important to understand what you're driving with each one. People will tell you that they have updated their product's control software - which is excellent, because now they have a new reason to grow. However, they assume the product coverage has now increased when really it hasn't. They have actually increased their hit rate. You have the same product effectively, only now when you demonstrate your product's capability to prospects, more of them will convert. You did not drive more people to see it – your salespeople did the same number of meetings; your quotes were the same. Just be aware that with any improvement to your business if no new opportunities were created then all you did was change hit rate.

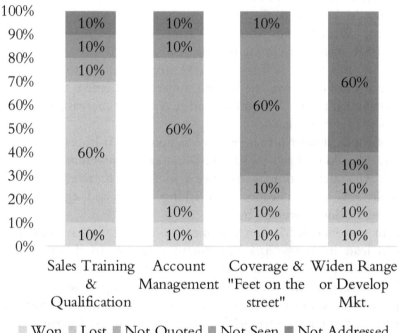

■ Won ■ Lost ■ Not Quoted ■ Not Seen ■ Not Addressed

Figure 12.2 – PPH$^{SM}$ gap analysis examples

PPH$^{SM}$ analysis will give you an accurate picture of your situation and help to drive your growth strategy. In Figure 12.2 we can see 5 examples which can be uncovered by analysis with some general actions from left to right.

- Low hit rate = Sales training & qualification
- Products never quoted to customers = Channel/account management
- Customers don't know your products = Coverage & feet on street
- Small addressable market = Widen range or develop market.

PPH$^{SM}$ analysis can be done at a global or country level. Much of this comes down to the differentiation between markets. For example, completing a PPH$^{SM}$ review for Germany and France separately may be more beneficial as the markets are likely to be different and so the PPH$^{SM}$ will look different. Whereas America could probably be considered as a single PPH$^{SM}$.

So why do I tell you all this? Well, these are your controls for the business. Which ones can sales have influence over and what SalesDISK$^©$ tactics are going to help you?

You can, and many will try, to make improvements to each part of your business; however, the biggest impact will come from impacting the smallest number. The impact on revenue by increasing one lever by 1% is 1/current share.

For example, if your hit rate is 30%, as figure 12.1 shows, growing hit rate 1% should lead to a 1/30= 3.3% increase in revenue.

This is why sales training is attractive as increasing hit rate by 1% sounds possible and a lot cheaper than asking R&D and engineering to increase product coverage by 1%.

If your presence is 5% and you increase it by 1% then your impact would lead to 1/5= 20% increase in revenue. In this case, really understanding if you need feet-on-the-street or channel management is the answer. Just show up more. Your largest impact will come from attacking the weakest lever. Product coverage changes can happen in 1-3 years, presence coverage can happen within 2-4 quarters and hit rate can have an impact 1-2 quarters.

So how does this tie to SalesDISK$^©$ and picking people and tactics? Although this can drive multiple business decisions, it also helped me as a VP of sales understand what I needed my team focused on, to get them to their challenging quotas or to really try to force some growth into the business.

DEVELOP is linked directly to hit-rate - think about it, listen better, convince better, demonstrate better, close better.

IDENTIFY is linked directly to presence. Here, simply be in front of more customers.

SERVICE links to both presence (be in front of customers) and hit rate (make them like you).

KNOWLEDGE links to hit rate (talks prospect's language) and presence (can be used to find the customers who need your solution).

| | DEVELOP | IDENTIFY | SERVICE | KNOWLEDGE |
|---|---|---|---|---|
| PPH Lever(s) | HIT RATE | PRESENCE | PRESENCE & HIT RATE | HIT Rate & PRESENCE |
| Symptoms | We're not winning enough deals; we're losing to competition | Pipeline is low, we don't see enough deals. We don't see enough business | Customers are swapping to competitors | We're not winning enough deals; Customers respect competitors more |
| Cause | Selling is not Compelling | Not enough opportunities are being identified | We are not delivering on promises post-sale | Selling is not compelling |

Figure 12.3 - Connection between segments & PPH levers

The PPH$^{SM}$ helps you understand where opportunities exist within chosen markets. Your answer can of course be to focus on other markets - this is fine, assess them using the same process.

It is common to look at the markets and assess efforts to be deployed. With some markets you simply choose to service the market and wind down effort as you see no large win, preferring to put efforts into other areas.

Some markets will only take you so far but what they may allow you to do is to get traction and an ability to grow to a position of dominance. With this set up and a position already created, it is much easier to move to associated markets and start to grow there, with a lot of the hard work done.

Some people revel in telling me how big their market is and therefore how big the opportunity is, but with such markets you may face existing players or find existing channel barriers are too hard to overcome.

So, what market should you be in - big or small? Well, it's the classic big fish/small pond, or small fish/big pond issue. What you have to admire is that, as we know, some big fish exist in big ponds so some people really did take the risk and 'go for it'.

A PPH$^{SM}$ analysis is also a really great way to look at acquisitions. If you can find a target with a high addressable market share, then you will not need to invest in initial R&D to make instant change. Presence and hit rate being much cheaper and faster to fix than engineering new market leading products.

PPH$^{SM}$ also helps us understand and rank the problems. For example, someone may assess our hit rate is low at 30% and think it's the number one problem. 30% hit rate is only a problem if you already have relatively high product coverage or presence. 30% hit rate could be completely fine and not need addressing as a problem if product and presence went up a few percent. Not that I'm saying don't be the best you can be, but there comes a point where polishing hit rate more, doesn't add as much as you would like.

Even if the hit rate was the answer, using the PPH$^{SM}$ structure forces you to focus all your thinking on tactics that increase hit rate.

The timescale to fix is critically important. Although you want to execute a SalesDISK$^©$ and not have it change (because you designed it that way), as the business changes it will naturally evolve, and as problems hit, it may also need short term warping.

Salespeople are different - not everyone can prospect, not everyone can demo - but as the historic comedy character Blackadder said, "Needs must when the devil vomits in your kettle."

Sometimes you just need to get with the short-term program to correct the business course or give it the needed jump-start. I recently spoke to a sales manager who told me 'salespeople need to be hired for attitude and then their direction can be changed as needed'. I partially agree. Good people always can do good things - they are especially good at short-term changes or evolution of change. But the direction-changes can only be so frequent, and they can only be by a few degrees. Changing them from direct sales to a dealer channel manager for example is a skill-set change.

It's better to start with a plan - any plan is better than no plan. Of course, good people with good attitudes help - it goes without saying. One of my favourite interview questions when hiring sales staff was "if I asked you to be in Manchester (or any location 4 hours away) at 9am tomorrow morning because we needed it, would that be a problem?" Interestingly this did kick out a lot of candidates. They would say "Why so early"? The ones we hired said something like, "it's not easy to do that but if it helps then I can."

As I write this, I can see the faces of all the people I asked this question to in my head - all have succeeded or are in the process of succeeding in sales. I feel tremendously proud to have been involved in their journey.

Problems do happen. You may think you don't have many, which is good, but trust me, you have some or they are coming. All of us have opportunities, gaps that we need to address, ways we can grow. No one can escape from thinking about opportunity. As noted before, if you're reading this it's because you want to be or are a leader. If you are, you own change and you own growth.

Find out more about PPH$^{SM}$ at FrankLynn.com and GaidoScientific.com

## CHAPTER SUMMARY

Businesses have both problems and opportunities.

Problems tend to show up as short-term - for example, we are going to miss revenue this quarter as the pipeline is too low. Opportunities tend to provide growth and also longer-term solutions to the problems.

Big problems are a threat to the continuation along your chosen path and they require immediate fixes.

Opportunities can be many and varied. They need to be identified and ranked to ensure the best investments of time and money.

PPH$^{SM}$ is a tool used to help understand market-share composition and the levers that drive your business's revenue.

PPH$^{SM}$ comprises a market value based on a definition of your choice - product coverage, presence (coverage & offer rate) and hit rate.

PPH$^{SM}$ helps identifies gaps and actions to be taken. The key is to make the largest impact using the smallest amount of effort.

PPH$^{SM}$ helps drive focus, and links directly to your SalesDISK$^{©}$. Missing pipeline? Focus on IDENTIFY. Hit rate is the problem? Focus on DEVELOP, etc

Salespeople will often need to change direction a little to help the business with problems. This causes a short-term change in their SalesDISK$^{©}$.

As the business evolves, to take advantage of new opportunities leaders need to either hire new salespeople with new SalesDISK$^{©}$s or update the SalesDISK$^{©}$s applying to existing staff.

# Chapter 13: The SalesDISK© Calculator

The purpose of SalesDISK© is to force thought and discussion around what your company's sales go-to-market strategy is, and to visualise it. The calculator is that visualisation. It takes discussion about needs and ownership, and makes it into a graphic to be discussed, debated, and finally issued to salespeople to set and drive focus.

The calculator is available at www.salesdisk.com along with a video tutorial and other resources.

There are in fact 3 calculators: the *Segment*, the *Subsegment* and the *Customised.*
Let's start with the *Segment* calculator. The *Segment* calculator works solely on the segment priority and ownership by department. It is the fastest way to drive a discussion between departments about ownership of elements within the sale.

| SEGMENT | Priority | Sales | Marketing | Other |
|---------|----------|-------|-----------|-------|
| DEVELOP | 40% | 80% | 20% | 0% |
| IDENTIFY | 30% | 50% | 50% | 0% |
| SERVICE | 10% | 10% | 0% | 90% |
| KNOWLEDGE | 20% | 20% | 80% | 0% |

Figure 13.1 – Example input for segment calculator

Error checkers are in place to ensure that the priority column adds up to 100% as does the service row (ignoring the priority %)
After completing the data entry, the user can select 2 options: update charts or spreadsheet.

*Spreadsheet* sends all the data to an excel file for download, allowing you to keep the values for later discussion.

*Create Charts* opens the chart control tab of the calculator. This creates a sunburst chart, defaulting to show the SalesDISK© from the salesperson's point of view. However, there are options to display the other departments (marketing and other).

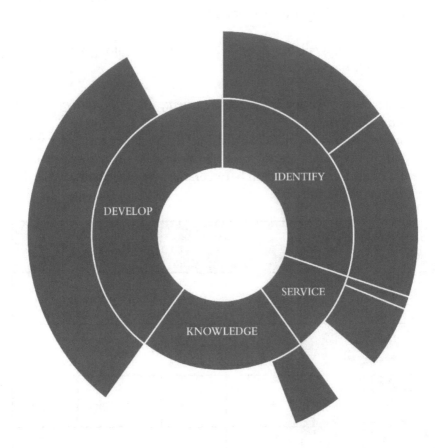

Figure 13.2 - SalesDISK© sunburst chart depicting the sale from the salesperson's view.

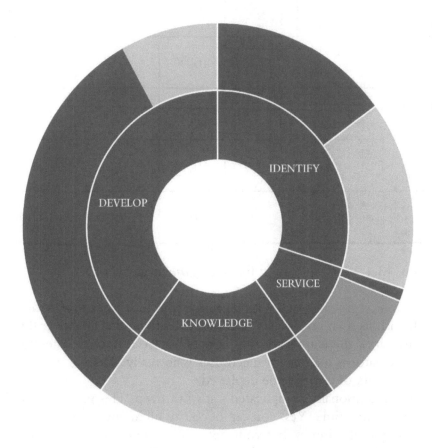

Figure 13.3 - SalesDISK© including additional departments (marketing & other) – www.salesdisk.com

The *Subsegment* calculator is to be used for more comprehensive reviews and allows you to assign responsibilities for specific subsegments tactics.

| Tactical Option | Priority | Sales | Marketing | Other |
|---|---|---|---|---|
| Lead Processing | 20% | 100% | 0% | 0% |
| Farming | 10% | 0% | 100% | 0% |
| Prospecting | 60% | 100% | 0% | 0% |
| Business Development | 20% | 30% | 70% | 0% |

Figure 13.4 – Example input for *Subsegment* calculator

With four segments, each with a priority and four subsegments, again each with its own priority, all of which need to be allocated over three departments, there are sixty-four controls to be reviewed. Therefore, this calculator is for the advanced user who really wants to work out the finer mix of tactics to be deployed.

It's not intentionally complicated - it's just deep. This process should take you some time. Yes, you can of course fill in your existing tactics in a couple of minutes, but your options – where you consider what you could do - require thought.

The *Customised* calculator is identical to the *Subsegment* calculator, but it allows you to allocate the tasks over 4 categories which replace departments. This could be salesperson, internal sales, applications person or simply Sally, Bob, and Dave.

Along with the segment starburst chart the *Subsegment* and *Customised* calculators deliver you the subsegment SalesDISK©

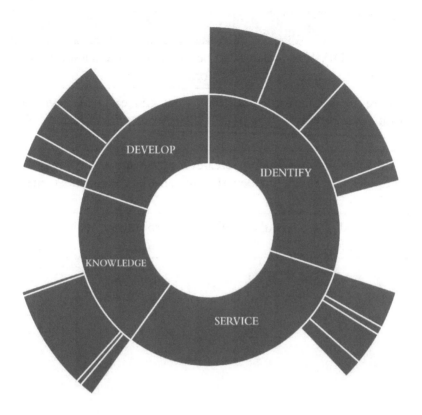

Figure 13.5 – Subsegment SalesDISK© sunburst chart. Departments and further labels can be turned on and off as required. Labels are also available through mouse hover.

## CHAPTER SUMMARY

The SalesDISK© calculator can be found at www.salesdisk.com along with a tutorial video and other resources.

There are 3 calculators. *Segment* (fast and easy) *Subsegment* (full review) and *Customised* (full review with customisable owners).

The SalesDISK© calculator creates a sunburst plot defaulted to the salespersons view. Departments and labels can be turned on/off as required.

The SalesDISK© calculator allows you to export your analysis as a .xlsx file.

# Afterword

Well done - you got here and not only that, you're reading the summary. I hope you enjoyed it. If you did, tell someone. If not keep it to yourself – I won't tell if you don't.

So, let's go back and think about the overall premise of the book - basically it's "think about it." Think about what is going on and what you're going to do about it. SalesDISK© is a tool yes but at its core it's a way of using aligned language and allowing you to lump ideas together, giving some structure to your thinking. You don't necessarily need to use the disk but you do need to do the thinking and be able to explain and defend your sales model based on decisions you have made. "It was like that when I got here" is not going to fly as an excuse. As noted, there are multiple ways to skin a cat, sometimes the obvious way works, keep doing what you're doing or do what your competitors are doing. However maybe, just maybe, you can try something new and possibly even re-define how sales work within your market. Maybe you can find the efficiency to increase profit, fund another project or just make everyone involved more focused and fulfilled. Maybe you use the model to massively increase your effectiveness, growing the business beyond its viewed potential.

The thinking never really stops but at some point, a decision should be made - you can change it later but unless you set a time to make that decision nothing will happen.

Ideas and change are worth chewing over. Some decisions should be made as if a gun is to your head, others should be considered, and time allocated away from life's busy work. The important ones will be reviewed in your head as you do the dishes, make the dinner, cut the lawn, and, critically, they develop during open and rambling discussions with stakeholders.

I have often found walking the simplest way of finding the time to talk - simply being unable to use a computer works. You have no choice but to circle the conversation until it gets exhausted. Alternatively, a coffee shop with just pen and paper or lastly a meeting room with a massive whiteboard - discussions always seem to flow faster when not in your normal environment.

If you can't think or the people around you don't want to think, then either do the thinking for them, ask a friend or consultant, or take it as a sign that there is more for you in this world and you may be better elsewhere.

Work is not stagnant; it's not like working a checkout at a grocery store, you don't just turn up and do the same every day. You're driving this thing buddy. Every day is for thinking and planning change. Remember, if you want to lead, then think, plan, and execute change - everything else is just arm waving or trains-on-time stuff.

Made in United States
Troutdale, OR
10/28/2023

14108440R00120